America's
Smithsonian

America's Smithsonian

Celebrating 150 Years

SMITHSONIAN INSTITUTION PRESS · Washington and London

For the *America's Smithsonian* Project

CURATORIAL COORDINATOR
Jeffrey L. Brodie

CURATORIAL PROJECT SPECIALISTS
Tracy L. Goldsmith
Chris Shaffer

PROJECT EDITOR
Kay Fleming

Abbreviations used in captions:

AAA	Archives of American Art
AM	Anacostia Museum
AMSG	Arthur M. Sackler Gallery
CC	Castle Collection
CH	Cooper-Hewitt, National Design Museum
HMSG	Hirshhorn Museum and Sculpture Garden
NASM	National Air and Space Museum
NMAA	National Museum of American Art
NMAfA	National Museum of African Art
NMAH	National Museum of American History
NMAI	National Museum of the American Indian
NMNH	National Museum of Natural History
NPG	National Portrait Gallery
NPM	National Postal Museum
RG	Renwick Gallery
SA	Smithsonian Institution Archives
SIL	Smithsonian Institution Libraries

For Smithsonian Institution Press
DIRECTOR: Daniel H. Goodwin
EDITORIAL DIRECTOR: Peter F. Cannell
EDITOR: Jack Kirshbaum
DESIGNER: Janice Wheeler
PRODUCTION MANAGER: Kenneth J. Sabol

Library of Congress Cataloging-in-Publication data available
ISBN 1-56098-697-2 (cloth); 1-56098-699-9 (paper)
Library of Congress Catalog Number 95-49181
British Library Cataloging-in-Publication data available

Manufactured in the United States of America
00 99 98 97 96   5 4 3 2

Color separations, printing, and binding by
R.R. Donnelley and Sons, Co., Willard, Ohio.
Special thanks to the prepress team: Scott Baker, Doris
Carney, Max Caywood, Travis Daniel, Bill Hammersmith,
Barb Hamons, Doug Heyman, Ron Heyman, Jeff Jacobs,
Tom Kempf, Nancy Kilgore, Dick Koser, Dave Lawrence,
Scott Meyers, Brian Phillips, Steve Shaver, Rusty Taylor, Jerry
Wechter, James Wilson, and Jerry Wright. Also, thanks to
Shirley Schulz and Cliff Mears.

∞ The paper used in this publication meets the minimum
requirements of the American National Standard for
Permanence of Paper for Printed Library Materials Z39.48-
1984.

COVER: Front design by Spiker Design and Wojnar
Productions. "Anthias Schooling / Red Sea" courtesy of
Jeffrey L. Rotman Photography. © Smithsonian Institution.
All rights reserved. Back photograph by Dane Penland,
90-6958.
FRONT MATTER ILLUSTRATIONS: American flag *(p. ii)*
and the Mall *(p. xii)*, photographs by Dane Penland, 83-9221,
79-13768.

For permission to reproduce any of the illustrations, please
correspond directly with the museum sources. The
Smithsonian Institution Press does not retain reproduction
rights for these illustrations individually or maintain a file
of addresses for photo sources.

The Smithsonian 150th Corporate Partner Program was created to assist the Institution with its marketing objectives and to secure funding for the America's Smithsonian exhibition. Through this innovative program, the "Proud Partners of the Smithsonian's 150th Anniversary Celebration" have generously contributed their staffs, their ideas, their expertise, and their financial support. It gives us great pleasure to acknowledge our corporate partners: *Discover® Card, Intel Corporation, MCI Communications Corporation,* and *Trans World Airlines, Inc.*

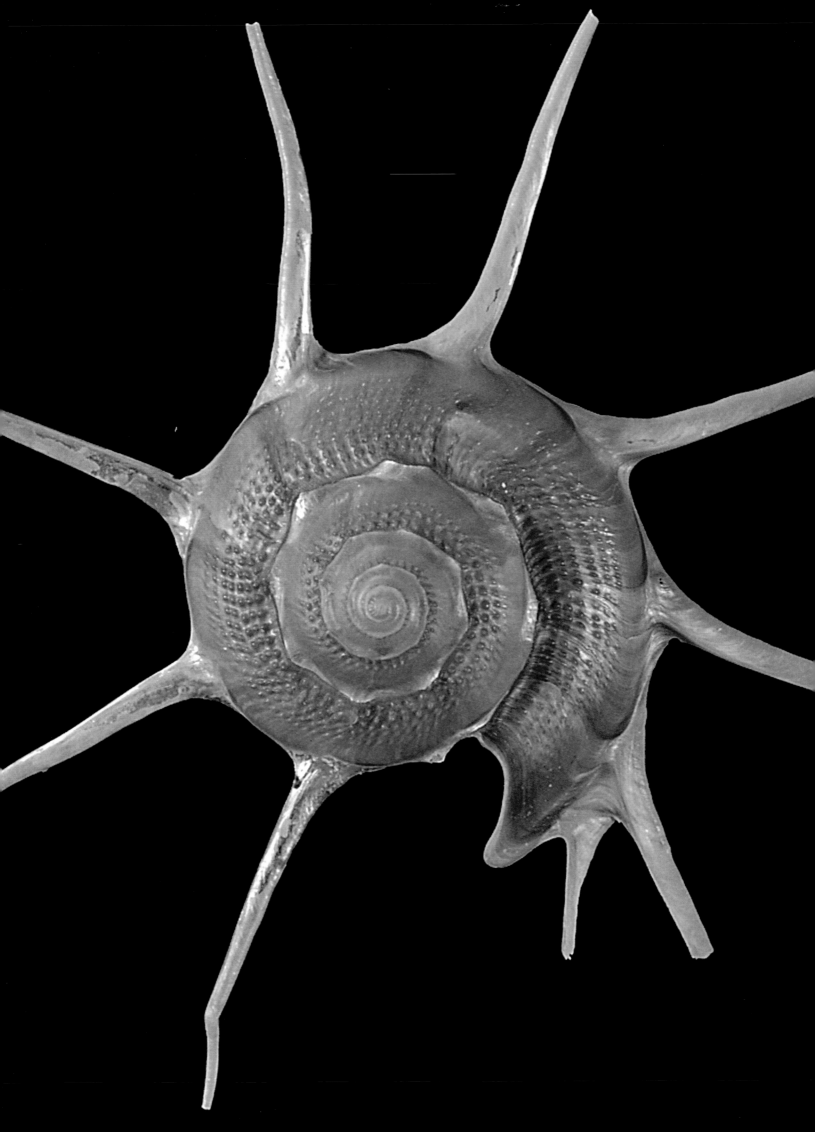

Contents

Foreword

In 1846, with a bequest from Englishman James Smithson, the United States Congress formally established the Smithsonian Institution in Washington, D.C. This gift carried enormous responsibilities and obligations. Smithson charged the United States with creating an institution that would serve the American people through the "increase and diffusion of knowledge."

Since its inception, the Smithsonian Institution has grown and developed to reflect and respond to the ever-changing needs of our society. Curators, scientists, and specialists conduct research in a multitude of disciplines and have collected more than 140 million objects—historic artifacts, scientific specimens, and works of art—held in trust for the American people. The Smithsonian's research facilities increase our knowledge of the oceans, continents, and galaxies of our universe. The Smithsonian shares this information through its museums, traveling exhibitions, computer on-line services, and educational outreach programs.

It is essential to make the Smithsonian's museums and research facilities as accessible to the American people as possible. It is often difficult for the American public to visit Washington, D.C., and explore the Smithsonian's world for themselves. Therefore, in celebration of our 150th anniversary, the Smithsonian Institution is pleased to bring its treasures to you.

I. Michael Heyman
Secretary

Preface

Soon after taking office in the fall of 1994, our new Secretary, I. Michael Heyman, announced his desire to share the celebration of the Smithsonian Institution's 150th anniversary with the American people. He wanted to take the Smithsonian "to the people," and thus was born *America's Smithsonian.*.

An entirely new exhibition, *America's Smithsonian* showcases some of the most important artifacts and icons from the many museums, archives, and research departments within the Institution. In fact, we believe it is the largest museum exhibition ever to travel around this country as well as the largest collection of national treasures ever exhibited outside of the Smithsonian. The exhibition is divided into three sections: Discovering, Imagining, and Remembering. Using these terms, our curators begin to suggest how objects become treasures and icons of personal and national significance.

Special efforts have been made to select objects that would appeal to the widest possible audience. Such an effort could not have been made possible without the extraordinary cooperation of literally hundreds of staff throughout the Institution. In particular, a special thanks is due to Constance Berry Newman, Under Secretary, for her able direction, her wise counsel, and her constant enthusiasm and support for this project.

J. Michael Carrigan
Director
America's Smithsonian

The Smithsonian Institution

A Brief History of Its Founding

THE SMITHSONIAN INSTITUTION

Founded in 1846 with funds provided by the bequest of James Smithson, the Smithsonian has a history that reflects a balance between the twin aims established for the Institution in Smithson's will: "the increase and diffusion of knowledge." Since the Institution's beginning, its leaders have interpreted the goals defined by James Smithson in different ways. The resulting balance between "increase"—collection, classification, and research—and "diffusion"—museum functions and other educational programs—remains a delicate one.

JAMES SMITHSON

James Smithson's father, Hugh, advanced through the ranks of English aristocracy largely due to his marriage to Elizabeth Percy, a member of a wealthy and noble family. Hugh adopted her surname of Percy, and King George III appointed him Duke of Northumberland.

In 1765 James Smithson, originally named James Lewis Macie, was born out of wedlock to Hugh Percy and Elizabeth Keate Macie. From 1782 to 1786, James distinguished himself at Pembroke College, Oxford, and inherited his mother's fortune in 1800. He discovered a carbonate of zinc in 1803, published many scholarly papers, and became a Fellow of the Royal Society in London. He adopted his father's original surname—becoming James Smithson—in 1806.

Despite his fortune and scientific reputation, his illegitimacy precluded him from assuming noble status in England. Perhaps his deeply felt resentment over this exclusion was in part responsible for his decision to write a will that would potentially leave his estate to the United States government. In his will, Smithson left his estate to his nephew, Henry James Hungerford. However, if Hungerford died childless, the entirety of the estate was to go

Young James Smithson in Oxford Attire

James Smithson (signature)

This intaglio engraving of James Smithson was prepared for the Smithsonian Institution based on a neoclassical bust in low relief attributed to the Italian artist Antonio Canova (1757–1822). The bust was discovered among Smithson's personal effects after his death. Some attribute the bust to French sculptor Nicolas Pierre Tiolier. NMAH

British gold sovereign, 1838. NMAH

to the U.S. government, "to found at Washington, under the name of the Smithsonian Institution, an Establishment for the increase and diffusion of knowledge among men." James Smithson died in 1829, and his estate was passed on to Mr. Hungerford.

THE SMITHSONIAN IS ESTABLISHED

James Smithson's nephew died without any heirs in 1835. Smithson's bequest was announced to Congress shortly thereafter. A great debate in Congress ensued, initially over whether to accept the bequest, and then over the exact nature of Smithson's intentions. Finally, on August 10, 1846, the 29th Congress passed the Bill of Incorporation of the Smithsonian Institution. Some congressmen envisioned a national university or an agricultural institute. Others were inclined to establish a national library, and there were also advocates of an astronomical observatory. One idea many shared was the establishment of a national museum.

In 1838 Richard Rush, President Andrew Jackson's representative, accompanied the bequest in the form of 105 bags of British gold sovereigns across the Atlantic. Worth about $500,000, almost all of the more than 100,000 sovereigns were melted down and restruck into United States gold coins. Two single pieces remained miraculously preserved by the U.S. Mint. They were deposited in the Smithsonian in June 1923, when the entire Mint collection was transferred to Washington. Those two sovereigns bear silent witness to a great act of generosity by an Englishman who had never set foot on American soil.

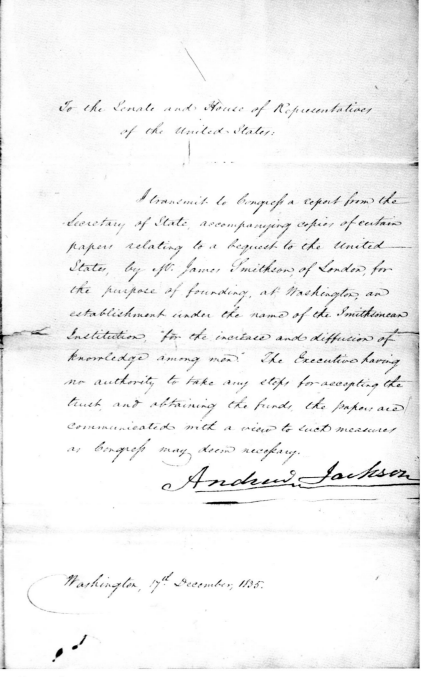

JOSEPH HENRY AND SPENCER BAIRD: THE ORIGINAL DIRECTION OF THE SMITHSONIAN INSTITUTION

Congress mandated that the Smithsonian be governed by a board of regents designated to choose a Secretary to head the new Institution, and that the Institution include a library, a museum, and an art

President Andrew
Jackson's letter notifying
the U.S. Senate and House
of Representatives of
James Smithson's bequest

1817 cast bronze portrait medal of James Smithson, made by French Mint engraver Nicolas P. Tiolier. It served as a model for the great seal of the Smithsonian Institution as well as the Smithson Medal, first presented at the James Smithson Bicentennial celebration in 1965. Some attribute the bust to Italian artist Antonio Canova. NMAH

BELOW: The Smithsonian mace—symbol of knowledge, freedom, and progress—is made of gold and silver with insets of diamonds, rubies, and Smithsonite. The lion figure atop the mace derives from the family coat of arms of Sir Hugh Smithson, father of James Smithson. CC

gallery. Beyond this, the direction of the Institution was largely to be determined by its own leadership.

The board of regents—composed of the vice-president, chief justice, three senators, three House members, and six citizens chosen at large—elected Joseph Henry, a physicist from Princeton University, the first Secretary of the Smithsonian Institution.

From 1846 to 1878, Joseph Henry focused his energies primarily on making the Smithsonian a preeminent research institution. He separated the public museum divisions from the research-oriented facets of the Institution—a split that culminated in moving the recently acquired U.S. government collections of the National Museum out of the Smithsonian Castle and into a separate building.

If Joseph Henry's ambitions were devoted to the "increase" of knowledge by emphasizing research, Spencer Fullerton Baird, the second Secretary of the Smithsonian Institution, was dedicated to its

The Arts & Industries Building, as the United States National Museum, shortly after its opening in 1881

THE SMITHSONIAN TODAY

Today the Smithsonian Institution pursues its mission to increase and diffuse knowledge, even as the Institution itself continues to evolve. Museums devoted to history, art, and design have opened. The Institution has become deeply involved in mounting traveling exhibitions, fostering research, conducting educational outreach programs, maintaining music and lecture programs, preserving archives, publishing, and supporting the Folklife program, including the Folkways record label. The National Zoological Park, the Smithsonian Tropical Research Institute, Smithsonian Astrophysical Observatory, and Smithsonian Environmental Research Center explore our world and beyond through in-depth field work and research. James Smithson's initial bequest has become a reality—a world of discovering, imagining, and remembering.

"diffusion." During his tenure as Secretary, from 1878 to 1887, Baird supervised the creation of a new National Museum Building, now known as the Arts and Industries Building. Furthermore, Baird redirected the Institution toward collections-based research rather than individual research, thus furthering the museum-related functions of the Smithsonian.

Introduction

Welcome to *America's Smithsonian*, an exhibition celebrating the 150th anniversary of the Smithsonian Institution! In 1827 James Smithson, an Englishman, wrote a will that eventually left his estate "to the United States of America, to found, at Washington, under the name of the Smithsonian Institution, an Establishment for the increase and diffusion of knowledge."

An act of Congress established the Smithsonian Institution in 1846. It is the world's largest museum complex and an international center for research. The Institution preserves more than 140 million objects in sixteen museums and several research facilities, archives, and libraries, and maintains living animals in the National Zoological Park. It is the nation's treasure house, reflecting the diversity and complexity of our world.

America's Smithsonian contains a selection of the Institution's most treasured objects. Each has a compelling story to tell. Many are testaments to significant historical events and unique human achievements. Some help us understand the everyday lives of past generations and remind us that the objects we use today will become treasures in the future. Others are works of incalculable artistic value, revealing the imagination and creativity of the human spirit. Still others aid us in discovering and solving nature's puzzles so that we can better understand our place within the physical universe.

James Smithson's bequest has developed into a place for discovering, imagining, and remembering. As such, the Smithsonian Institution performs an essential role in the cultural and scientific life of our nation. It embodies the desire of all Americans to commemorate their experiences, to savor objects of extraordinary beauty, and to acquire greater understanding of ourselves and the world around us. It furthers our collective search for greater knowledge and enriched experience.

Discovering

The Smithsonian has always been a center for scientific research focused on discovering the nature of the physical world and the forms of life inhabiting it. James Smithson's personal collections and those of 19th-century United States exploratory expeditions—which gathered specimens of plants, animals, fossils, minerals, and artifacts throughout the world—provided the foundations of the Smithsonian Institution's vast scientific collections.

Today the Institution holds more than 63 million scientific specimens. Paleontologists, zoologists, and botanists study fossils, animals, and plants to reveal the origins, structures, functions, and relationships of living things. Geologists and other specialists in the earth sciences analyze rocks and minerals to unravel the history of the solar system and to learn about the physical structure of our planet.

Our pursuit of scientific knowledge has intensified during the 20th century as new technologies have expanded the frontiers of discovery. We can now delve ever deeper into the earth and its oceans and travel ever further into space. The Smithsonian Institution's collections continue to grow to reflect these new avenues of discovery.

Detail of smithsonite
specimens.

Imprints of the Past

The solar system began to form at least 4.6 billion years ago. The oldest-known life forms were present about 3.5 billion years ago. Many times more species have evolved, flourished, and fallen into extinction than are alive on our planet today. Modern human beings, *Homo sapiens sapiens,* have existed for less than 130,000 years—a relative millisecond in the history of the universe.

Given such vast stretches of time and such complicated patterns of change, we have only begun to discover the history of life and of our own physical origins by learning how to analyze the clues contained in the earth. Our world is a gigantic book, written slowly over enormous stretches of time. We can still only partially interpret the signs it contains.

Some of our planet's rocks have preserved intriguing fossilized traces of earlier life forms. These fossils record the origin, proliferation, evolution, way of living, and extinction of plant and animal species over millions of years. Museum field expeditions have scraped, chiseled, and brushed away the mantle of rocks and time to reveal delicate impressions of life's past. From fossils as small as pollen grains and as large as *Tyrannosaurus rex,* paleontologists read our planet's shifting geological history, uncover the beginnings of our own species, and discover the dynamic patterns of change that propel us toward our future.

Carcharodon megalodon was a gigantic predator. The body stretching behind these ferocious 8-foot jaws reached about 40 feet in length—almost twice the length of its closest living relative, the great white shark. A swift, streamlined, voracious hunter like its modern descendants, *Carcharodon* lived between 5 million and 1.6 million years ago, about the time when human ancestors began roaming Africa.

Few fossilized remains of prehistoric sharks exist because their skeletons were formed of cartilage, a material far less durable than bone. Paleontologists have gleaned knowledge about *Carcharodon* and other early sharks primarily from their teeth, which have survived because they are composed of a bonelike substance coated with very hard enamel.

Fossil shark teeth, *Carcharodon megalodon,* Pliocene epoch, about 4.5 million years old (outer row of fossil teeth and inner rows of plastic casts set in reconstructed fiberglass jaws). NMNH

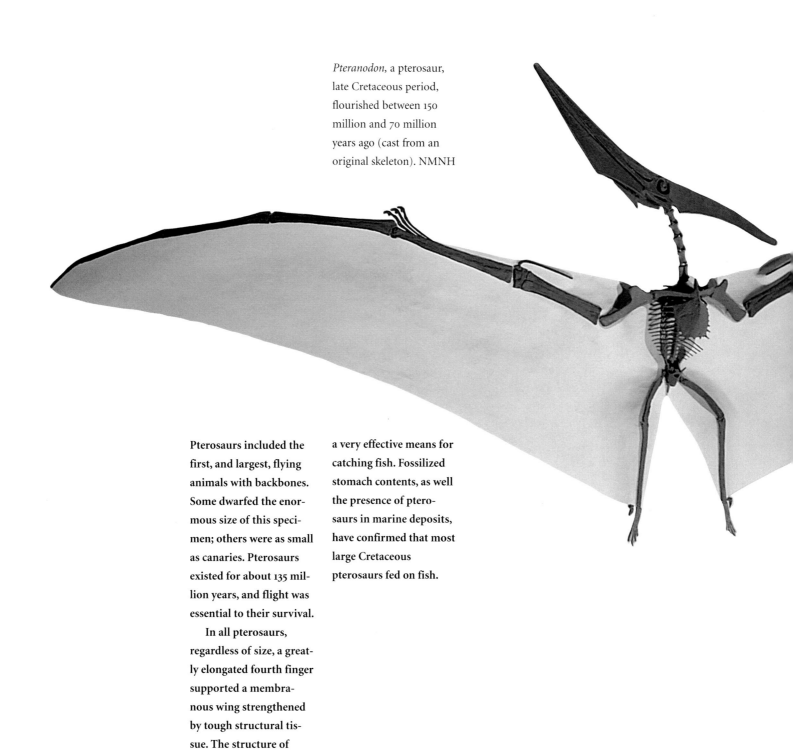

Pteranodon, a pterosaur, late Cretaceous period, flourished between 150 million and 70 million years ago (cast from an original skeleton). NMNH

Pterosaurs included the first, and largest, flying animals with backbones. Some dwarfed the enormous size of this specimen; others were as small as canaries. Pterosaurs existed for about 135 million years, and flight was essential to their survival.

In all pterosaurs, regardless of size, a greatly elongated fourth finger supported a membranous wing strengthened by tough structural tissue. The structure of pterosaurs' jaws and teeth provided them with a very effective means for catching fish. Fossilized stomach contents, as well the presence of pterosaurs in marine deposits, have confirmed that most large Cretaceous pterosaurs fed on fish.

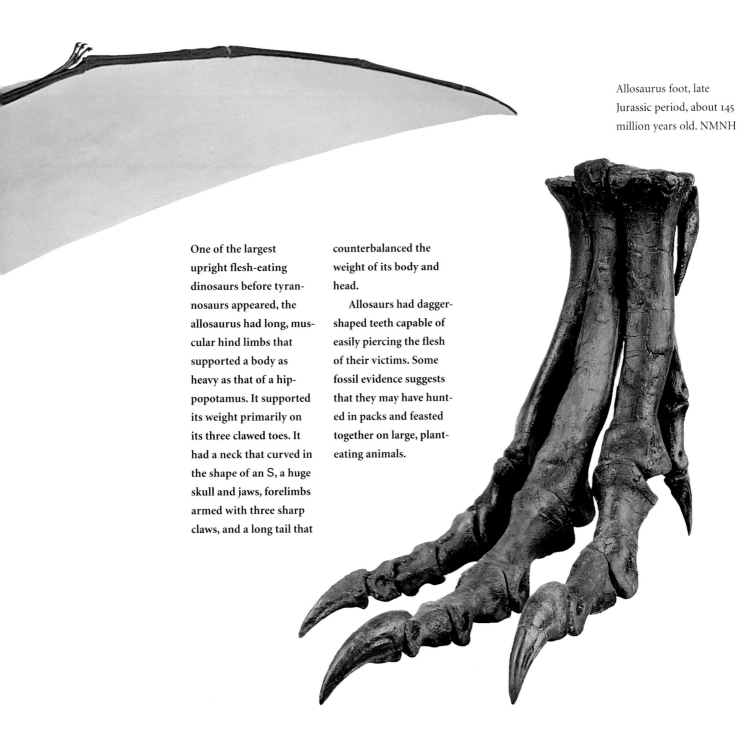

Allosaurus foot, late Jurassic period, about 145 million years old. NMNH

One of the largest upright flesh-eating dinosaurs before tyrannosaurs appeared, the allosaurus had long, muscular hind limbs that supported a body as heavy as that of a hippopotamus. It supported its weight primarily on its three clawed toes. It had a neck that curved in the shape of an S, a huge skull and jaws, forelimbs armed with three sharp claws, and a long tail that counterbalanced the weight of its body and head.

Allosaurs had dagger-shaped teeth capable of easily piercing the flesh of their victims. Some fossil evidence suggests that they may have hunted in packs and feasted together on large, plant-eating animals.

TRILOBITES AND AMMONITES

Trilobites were among the first animals to possess a somewhat flexible outer skeleton composed of chitin for body support. Their jointed legs identify them as members of the phylum Arthropoda, one of the most successful and diverse of all animal phyla. The phylum includes, among others, modern spiders and insects.

Trilobites' jointed legs and segmented outer skeletons, periodically shed to allow for growth, gave them distinct advantages in mobility, self-protection, and feeding. They evolved rapidly into several thousand genera and more than 10,000 species, and they dominated the shallow Cambrian seas for 20 million years, between 530 million and 510 million years ago.

At the end of the Cambrian period, trilobites unexpectedly went into sharp decline. Perhaps other animals evolved to compete with them for food. Or perhaps environmental changes affected them. A few trilobite lineages persisted through the Paleozoic, but the entire group became extinct about 250 million years ago.

Ammonites first appeared during the Permian period, and by the late Triassic they had begun playing key roles as swimming predators. They were hunted, in turn, by seagoing reptiles. Relatives of the modern nautilus, they died out some 65 million years ago.

Ammonites have been preserved in three principal ways. Sometimes their shells remained intact, rendered pristine white, pearly, or opalescent by chemical processes. Ancient ocean sediment sometimes preserved imprints of their shells. In other cases, sediment accumulated on the ocean floors, covering ammonites' dead shells and eventually crushing them with its weight. The different forms of preservation tell us much about the environmental conditions under which these animals died and became buried.

CENTER: Fossil Ammonite *(Arietites stellaris)*, Jurassic period, from about 188 million to about 184 million years old.

TOP LEFT: Fossil molars, mammoth *(Mammuthus* sp.), Pleistocene epoch, lived from more than 1.7 million years ago until possibly 4,000 years ago.

BOTTOM LEFT: Fossil molars, mastodon *(Mammut americanum)*, Pleistocene epoch, lived from more than 1.7 million years ago until possibly 8,000 years ago.

TOP RIGHT: Trilobite *(Isotelus latus)*, Ordovician period, about 450 million years old.

BOTTOM RIGHT: Trilobite in shale *(Modocia typicalis)*, Cambrian period, more than 520 million years old. All NMNH

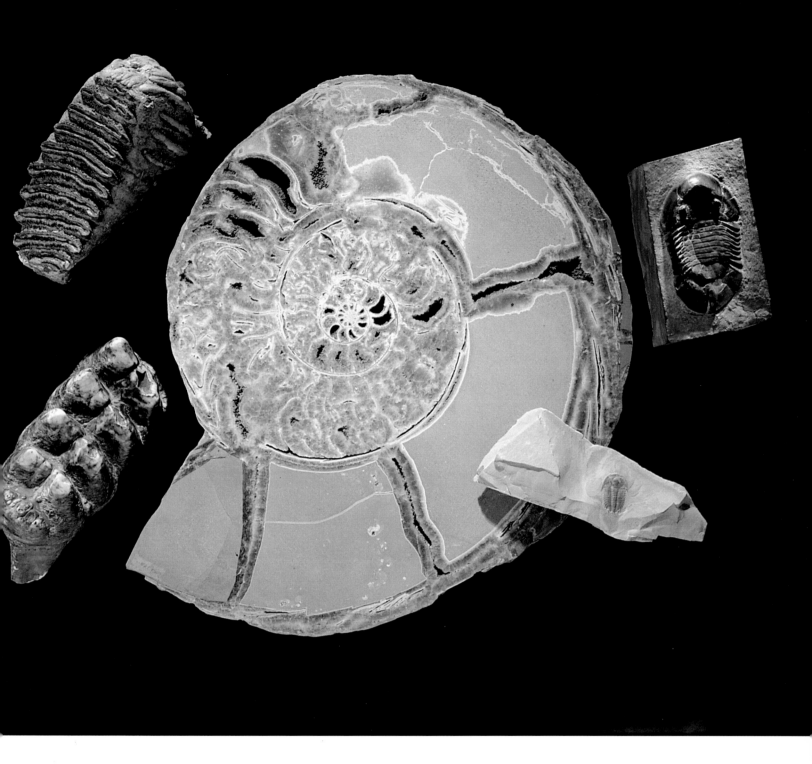

MASTODON AND MAMMOTH TEETH

Though linked by a common ancestor and of somewhat similar appearance, mastodons and mammoths had distinctive teeth adapted for different feeding strategies.

Mastodons were browsers. *Mastodon* means *breast-toothed,* referring to the four cone-shaped cusps of the molars with enamel-covered crowns that the animals possessed at one time. Their teeth were ideal for chewing the leaves, branches, and twigs gathered by their trunks. Though *Mammut* had only upper tusks, some earlier mastodons had both upper and lower tusks. Mastodons' upper tusks were shorter and less curved than those of mammoths.

Mammoths were grazers. Their molars had ridges, ideal for grinding coarse grasses. Mammoths had upper tusks weighing up to 350 pounds (130 kilograms) per pair and growing as long as 16 feet, 5 inches (about 5 meters). Their tusks were probably used for defense and for clearing snow away.

Both mammals lived during the Pleistocene epoch and became the prey of *Homo erectus* and *Homo sapiens* (including Neanderthals). Mastodons probably did not die out until after the last Ice Age had ended about 10,000 years ago. Mammoths are known from as recently as 4,000 years ago. Some of their fossilized remains have allowed scientists to discover much about the hunting habits and diets of ancient modern humans and their close relatives. One Smithsonian scientist has discovered mammoth kill sites almost 40,000 years old that contain butchering tools fashioned by yet-unidentified peoples.

Belemnites and Ammonites

These mobile mollusks cruised the Mesozoic seas. Some belemnites possessed straight, internal shells, whereas others lacked shells altogether. Most ammonites had coiled shells, although a few possessed straight ones. Both belemnites and ammonites had large brains and keen eyes. Their tentacles could grab smaller creatures and thrust the prey into their beaklike jaws.

Both groups swam swiftly backwards by squirting water through a funnel that pointed forward. Yet despite their skills as jet-propelled swimmers, they sometimes succumbed to swifter, shell-crushing predators. Belemnites and ammonites became extinct about 65 million years ago. The cause of their disappearance remains unknown.

Slab containing fossil crinoids *(Pentacrinus sub-angularis),* Jurassic period, between 203 million and 185 million years old. NMNH

Flower-shaped crinoids blanketed the seas peri-odically for more than 440 million years and are still with us today. Crinoids collect food with their arms. Each arm has a double row of tiny hollow appendages, known as tube feet, lining a mucus tract that runs up to its mouth. When a crinoid feeds, it extends its arms to catch food particles and moves them, via its tube feet, up its sticky food groove.

Ancient and modern crinoids' menu is limited to a broth of organic par-ticles and small organ-isms suspended in seawa-ter. Crinoids' highly spe-cialized anatomical struc-tures and behavior have allowed them to make the most of the rich marine soup.

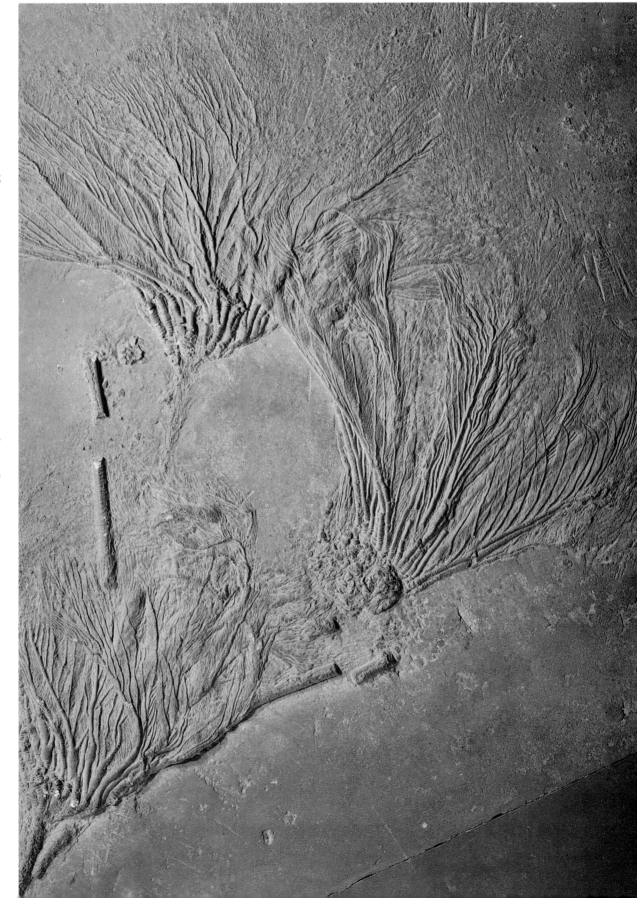

The Dinosaurs' Reign

Dinosaurs were the first large land vertebrates to walk on their toes with their feet directly underneath their bodies. They had hinged ankle joints, a buttressing shelf above their hip sockets, and an enlarged ridge along their thigh bones that helped strengthen their legs. These innovations allowed dinosaurs to travel vast distances. Their mobility was one of the principal reasons behind the dinosaurs' extraordinary success.

The dinosaurs were the largest land animals that ever lived. From about 225 million to 65 million years ago—roughly 160 million years—they were one of the planet's most numerous and varied land vertebrates. Except for some of the arthropods, especially the insects, few other groups of higher animals have matched the dinosaurs' longevity. Discovering their fossils, examining their biodiversity, and contemplating their size accounts for our unending fascination with these "fearfully great reptiles."

Members of the hadrosaur family, duckbills had skulls with elaborate, usually hollow, crests. Research has shown that some served as resonating chambers, enhancing the animals' vocalizations. Other studies suggest that they could have functioned as visual aids to species recognition.

Duckbills derive their common name from the unusual shape of their snouts. The front part of their jaws is flattened and toothless, but the rear portion is extremely long and contains multiple rows of teeth. Some duckbills had as many as 700 tightly packed teeth. These teeth provided them with a large shearing surface and enabled them to eat much tougher plants than most other animals could. Duckbills may have owed their success to their ability to eat what other plant eaters could not.

Duckbills were abundant during the late Cretaceous period. But their lack of defensive armor made them easy prey for big flesh eaters, like tyrannosaurs, whenever they strayed from their herds.

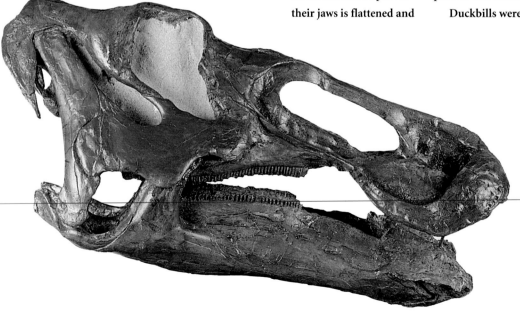

Skull of a duck-billed dinosaur (*Edmontosaurus regalis*), late Cretaceous period, flourished between 80 million and 65 million years ago (cast from an original skeleton). NMNH

The archaeopteryx is the oldest-known fossil bird. It possessed reptilian and avian features, and provides paleontologists with clues about the evolutionary relationship between dinosaurs and modern birds.

The ability to fly and other anatomical features—especially feathers and a distinctly birdlike wishbone, or furcula—separate the archaeopteryx from reptiles. Its feathers were asymmetric, indicating that it was capable of powered flight. But its chest muscles were neither as well developed nor as strong as those of modern birds. We also do not know whether the animal possessed the powerful four-chambered heart that modern birds have.

The archaeopteryx held many features in common with certain small, flesh-eating dinosaurs, including the shape of its skull, the small, sharply pointed teeth lining its jaws, and the structures of its hips, legs, and tail. These characteristics reveal its evolutionary link with dinosaurs.

BELOW: The diplodocus was one of the longest dinosaurs, measuring up to about 89 feet (27 meters), but it was extremely light for its size, weighing only about 12 tons. We can contrast its size-to-weight ratio with that of the modern blue whale, also about 90 feet long but weighing some 135 tons. *Diplodocus* was unusually light because it had a very slender, long tail and neck, as well as a comparatively tiny head.

This crushed skull typifies the condition in which paleontologists usually discover dinosaur bones. They "read" the fragmentary evidence, attempt to reconstruct the animals based upon the evidence provided by more complete articulated skeletons, and make educated guesses about their ways of life.

The small size of the diplodocus's slender, peg-like teeth shows that it was a plant eater. The teeth of most members of the genus also usually show a great deal of wear, indicating that they ate tough, fibrous food.

Archaeopteryx lithographica, Jurassic period, about 145 million years old (cast from an original skeleton). NMNH

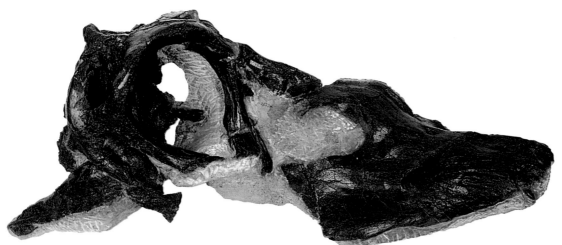

Skull of *Diplodocus longus,* Jurassic period, about 145 million years old. NMNH

SUSPENDED IN TIME

Whence we see spiders, flies, or ants entombed preserved forever in amber, a more than royal tomb.

—FRANCIS BACON

It is difficult for paleontologists to read the geologic history of spiders and insects. The fossil record is poor because these animals are usually soft-bodied and decay rapidly after death. It is equally difficult for paleontologists to study the forms of delicate body parts, like feathers and fur, because they decay rapidly after an animal dies.

But there is a natural preservative that helps scientists "read" the history of such fragile specimens—amber, or fossilized tree resin. Prehistoric insects, spiders, and the parts of some other organisms sometimes became trapped in sticky resin, and thus remained preserved intact when the resin hardened into amber.

Spider (Family Theridiidae) in amber, Tertiary period, 30 million to 25 million years old. NMNH

Spiders' exterior skeletons are not as hard as those of other arthropods and most insects. As a result, we have discovered little of their fossil record. This ancient spider is one of the rare few preserved in amber.

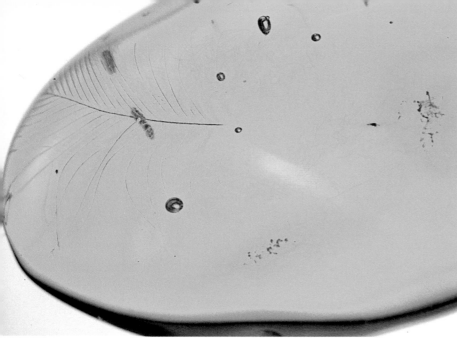

Feather (Family Picidae) in amber, Tertiary period, 30 million to 25 million years old. NMNH

Fossil feathers are very rare. This one has characteristics that permitted one scientist to identify it as belonging to a member of the woodpecker and flicker family. Discovered in the Dominican Republic, this is the oldest-known fossil of a New World woodpecker.

Termite (*Nasutitermes,* Family Termitidae) in amber, Lower Miocene period, about 23 million years old. NMNH

Termites have a better fossil record than most other insects. Not only has amber preserved them, but so has petrified wood, which sometimes contains traces of their nests and galleries.

This ancient, legume-bearing tree preserved parts of itself—its leaf and flower—in its own resin. Members of the *Hymenaea* genus still exist.

Tree leaf (*Hymenaea* sp.) in amber, Tertiary period, about 40 million years old. NMNH

15

The Evolving Earth

Geographic features seemingly as permanent as mountains change constantly. Continents—features riding atop the giant plates that make up the earth's crust—have shifted dramatically over time. During the average person's sixty-year life span, North America and Africa move further apart by about 6 feet. We are the inhabitants of an evolving planet.

Like fossils, minerals and rocks have recorded the long-term dynamics of the earth. They are the hieroglyphs that geologists decipher in order to read about our planet's history. Some have preserved traces of not only the movement of the continents, but also the short-term events, like volcanic activity, that formed them ages ago.

Our planet has also been bombarded by meteorites—some that fell on the planet relatively soon after the solar system had formed about 4.5 million years ago, and others that have hit the planet during our own lifetimes. These ancient fragments provide us with evidence about the formation of the solar system and the composition of other planets. Thus our planet has not only recorded its own history, but also preserved traces of the larger history of the solar system.

MINERALS, CRYSTALS, AND GEMS: REVEALING EARTH'S HISTORY

Minerals are solid, inorganic materials with specific chemical compositions and distinct internal structures. When minerals form inside the earth, their atoms lock together to create crystals. Under the right conditions and given sufficient space, crystals can "grow" into regular geometric forms with smooth surfaces. Depending upon their atomic structure and pattern of growth, they can aquire a wide range of spectacular shapes.

The atomic arrangement of a mineral crystal depends not only upon its chemical composition but also upon external forces. For example, pure carbon commonly crystallizes as graphite, one of the softest minerals and the component of pencil leads. But tremendous pressure and heat can transform carbon's crystal structure so that it forms diamonds, the hardest of all minerals. Thus some minerals can betray the circumstances of their own origins and allow us to discover more about the history of our planet and the forces that shaped it.

Gems are cut and polished mineral crystals prized for their beauty, durability, and rarity. We commonly stretch the definition of *gem* to include some beautiful and durable organic substances, like pearls, amber, jet, and coral. What determines the value of a gem is somewhat subjective, since our perceptions of what is beautiful and precious change over time.

The colors of minerals and gems result from light interacting with the different atoms that compose their crystals.

The mineral beryl is formed from atoms of beryllium, aluminum, silicon, and oxygen locked together into crystals. In its pure state, beryl is colorless. It acquires different colors, and names, when its crystals trap the atoms of other elements while they grow.

Chromium, and more rarely vanadium, produce the vibrant green of emeralds, the finest of which come from Colombia.

Beryl, emerald, Colombia.
NMNH

Beryl, emerald, North
Carolina. NMNH

Beryl, red beryl, Utah.
NMNH

Aquamarine exhibits the delicate, variable tints of the sea because iron is present in its crystals. Red is the rarest of all varieties of beryl, discovered only in Utah and New Mexico. Traces of manganese produce its intense red hue.

Beryl, aquamarine with muscovite, Pakistan.
NMNH

The intense blue of this specimen of azurite reveals the presence of copper in its atomic structure. The purity of its color is so compelling that Renaissance artists routinely ground azurite into powder for paint pigment. But moisture and oils in the paint alter the chemical composition of azurite, transforming it into the green mineral malachite. This is the reason many old masterpieces exhibit a greenish tint.

Azurite, Namibia. NMNH

Barite is the major ore of barium, the compounds of which are used to color fireworks green. Barium is also one of the ingredients in the "milkshakes" patients drink to highlight their digestive tracts for X rays. Barite itself is added to drilling muds when oil wells are drilled because its density helps support the sides of drill holes.

Dioptase, Namibia. NMNH

Dioptase contains copper, the source of its deep green hue. Mineral collectors prize its distinctive crystals. The mineral's name is coined from the Greek *diopteia,* "to see through."

19

The beauty of malachite results not only from the copper that gives it its green color, but also from the patterned bands that form when layers of microscopic crystals grow on top of each other. Each band consists of crystals of a different size. Smaller crystals produce lighter shades, and coarser crystals yield darker ones.

Crystals of minerals in the tourmaline family occur in a wide range of colors—from black to many shades of red, green, yellow, and blue. The colors result from the presence of different trace elements. The best gem-quality red and green tourmalines come from Brazil, Maine, and California.

Opals are not crystalline solids. They combine orderly, stacked arrangements of tiny silica spheres with water. The silica spheres diffract light and produce brilliant plays of color. Between 6 and 10 percent of an opal's weight comes from water. Most gem-quality opals come from Australia, but some spectacular examples originate in Nevada's Virgin Valley.

Liddicoatite (tourmaline family), Madagascar. NMNH

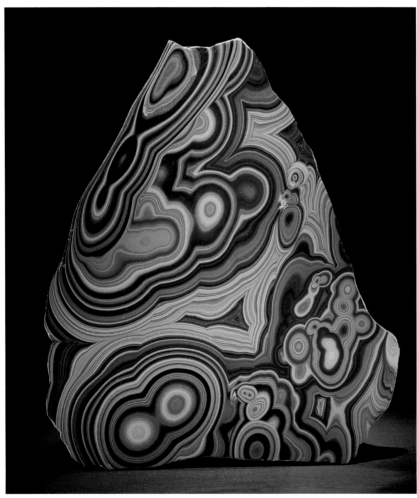

Malachite, Zaire. NMNH

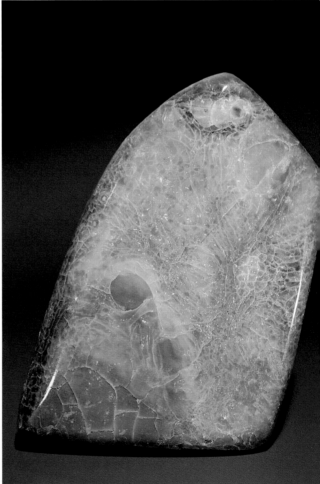

Opal, Nevada. NMNH

Calcite and aragonite in a
septarian nodule, Utah.
NMNH

A mud ball dried, cracked,
and solidified millions of
years ago to form this septarian nodule. Yellow calcite and dark brown arag-
onite crystallized from
water seeping into the
mud ball's cracks and created the pattern visible in
this specimen.

MINERALS AND AMERICAN HISTORY

Wulfenite crystal, Arizona.
NMNH

Wulfenite is a minor ore of lead and molybdenum. Americans mined wulfenites along with silver at the Red Cloud Mine in Arizona continuously from the 1860s until 1890, and then sporadically until 1941. Deep orange-red colors, along with unusual size and perfection, make Red Cloud wulfenites among the finest in the world.

The United States Postal Service often issues stamp series to commemorate different aspects of our American heritage. For each, it issues a special set of "First Day Covers," prized by collectors, on the date the series becomes available to the public.

The 1992 Mineral Heritage Stamp series paid tribute to our country's vast mineral wealth. The postal service based all of the stamps on photographs of mineral specimens preserved in the Smithsonian Institution.

The mineral specimens photographed for the heritage series reveal the impact that geological processes had on the patterns of exploration, immigration, and settlement in 19th-century America. News of huge mineral finds brought immigrants streaming into the country. The discovery of rich deposits of gold, silver, lead, zinc, and copper hastened the settlement of many western states.

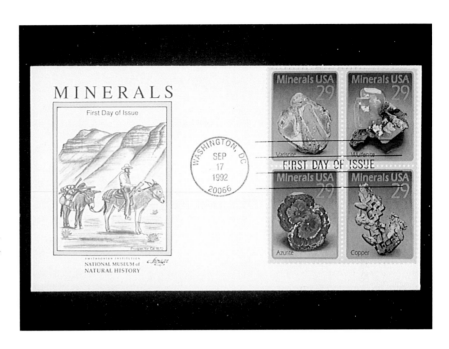

This copper specimen comes from Upper Michigan, North America's largest producer of copper from 1850 to 1887. Michigan mines were responsible for one of the first great immigrations of miners and mining engineers to this country. By 1893 the United States had become the world's greatest copper producer, thanks largely to the Michigan copper mines.

Among the first miners in U.S. territory were Native Americans who lived in what is now northern Michigan. They mined native copper as long as 5,000 years ago and pounded it into axes, knives, spear points, and fishhooks. Archaeologists have discovered thousands of ancient mining pits and remnants of stone hammers and other mining tools in Michigan.

Copper, Michigan.
NMNH

Azurite's rich blue color comes from copper, and most specimens have been discovered in copper mines. This specimen came from the Copper Queen Mine in Bisbee, Arizona. The mines there were most active between 1877 and 1975, when more than 7.7 billion pounds of copper were mined. The history of these mines reflects the growth of the west from the late 19th through the 20th centuries.

Variscite nodule (sliced and polished), Utah. NMNH

Unlike the others in this group, variscite is not an ore mineral—one mined for useful metals like copper or iron. Variscite is one of the more colorful American ornamental minerals, often fashioned into jewelry. Most major museums and private mineral collections throughout the world contain specimens of Utah variscite.

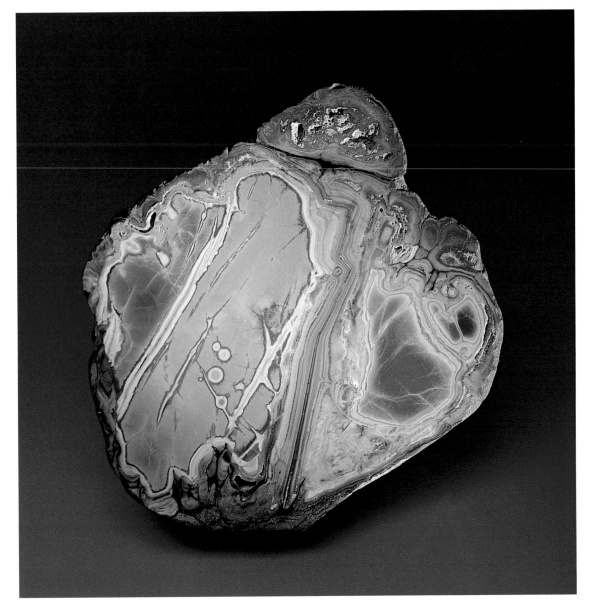

Smithsonite, one specimen from Greece *(left)* and two from Namibia. NMNH

DISCOVERING NEW MINERALS: JAMES SMITHSON

The mineral smithsonite is composed of zinc carbonate. Like beryl and many other minerals, its color depends on the presence of certain trace elements. Cobalt colors smithsonite pink, whereas copper makes it green or blue.

Smithsonite is named after James Smithson, the founder of the Smithsonian Institution. He first recognized it as a carbonate of zinc in 1802. He gave a lecture explaining his discovery to the Royal Society in London on November 18, 1802, and published his findings in the society's journal in 1803. The French mineralogist François Salpice Beudant officially named the mineral in Smithson's honor in 1832.

FLUORESCENT: MINERALS THAT GLOW IN THE DARK

Fluorescence refers to the visible light given off by materials exposed to invisible ultraviolet light. Most minerals do not fluoresce, but a few contain atoms in which electrons become boosted to a higher energy level by ultraviolet light. When the electrons fall back to their original level, they give off energy in the form of visible light.

CLOCKWISE FROM LEFT: Calcite, Texas; esperite (yellow) with hardystonite (purple), New Jersey; scheelite, Malay; clinohedrite (orange) and willemite (green) with bustamite, New Jersey; fluorite, Ohio. NMNH

CLOCKWISE FROM TOP LEFT: Willemite (green) with calcite (red), New Jersey; willemite, New Jersey; calcite, Morocco; fluorite (blue) with siderite, England; opal, North Carolina. NMNH

FROM LEFT: Sodalite, Canada; scapolite (wernerite), Canada. NMNH

TRANSFORMING EARTH'S TREASURES

We can shape any of the nearly 4,000 known minerals into gems, if crystals of sufficient size and quality are found, and if a craftsperson has the imagination and skill to reveal their hidden beauty. But we commonly use only about 15 different minerals to create gemstones because they combine desirable visual effects with hardness and availability.

We measure gems by their weight in carats. One metric carat equals .007 ounce (.2 gram). *Carat* comes from *carob,* a Mediterranean tree. For centuries, people used its seeds as a means for weighing precious stones.

Beauty, rarity, durability, and size are the basic criteria determining the value of a gemstone. A few gems have acquired a rich history that adds to their value, and some come from famous locales that make them especially desirable. Fluctuating fashions and market interests also play a role in determining the value of gems.

Spodumene (kunzite) crystal, California. NMNH

Because its crystals are sometimes quite large, gemologists can cut specimens of kunzite into particularly beautiful, large-faceted gems. Many deeply colored minerals with smaller crystals can appear too dark, and thus lose their beauty, when they are cut into large-faceted gems. But because kunzite is a rather pale pink, its color intensifies when it is cut into large forms.

This 12,445-carat topaz came from Brazil. In its pure state, topaz is colorless, but trace elements, radiation, and defects in crystal structure can produce a variety of hues. Pale golden brown is the most common. Deep golden orange, known as imperial topaz, is the most prized, and pink topaz the most rare.

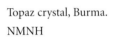

Topaz forms some of the largest gem-quality crystals of any mineral. Specimens weighing more than 600 pounds have been discovered. The most precious gems are those with deep golden hues. Although the majority of topazes are either colorless or pale, gemologists have learned how to manipulate the gem's color. In the early 1970s, blue topaz began to appear on the market and became popular. Gemologists created the shade by irradiating and heating colorless topaz.

Large balls of jadeite, known as *cobbles*, are frequently found in stream beds in certain parts of the world. Exposure to the elements weathers the outer surface, creating a rind. Dealers test the quality of cobbles by notching their rinds to expose small patches of jadeite inside.

Traces of iron and chromium produce jadeite's green color. Other elements impart a range of hues, from lavender through brown to almost black. Pure jadeite is white.

Jadeite cobble, Burma.
NMNH

Jadeite carving, Burma.
NMNH

Jade is a term for two
types of rock composed
of different minerals—
nephrite and the rarer
jadeite. Nephrite has a
silky appearance result-
ing from the interweav-
ing of feathery crystals.
Its colors range from
green to gray to milky
white. Jadeite, however, is
composed of tiny, blocky
crystals that give it a sug-
ary texture. It may be
white, orange, brown, or
even lilac, but its most
prized color is translu-
cent emerald green.

Even though nephrite
and jadeite are different
minerals, they both form
rocks that are very tough.
This toughness permits
artisans to shape both
into elaborate forms, like
this example, and to give
them a high polish.

Discovering the Origins of Our Solar System

The solar system began to form about 4.5 billion years ago. The oldest known earth rock is about 4 billion years old. A huge chapter of Earth's history—about 500 million years—is missing from its own natural record. Meteorites have fallen continuously on our planet since the solar system first formed, and they provide us with clues about what happened during those missing years. Radioactive dating has shown us that many meteorites are hundreds of millions of years older than the oldest-known earth rocks, including some that are about as old as the solar system itself.

Most meteorites originate in the asteroid belt. Some are fragments of large asteroids that formed and were destroyed early in the solar system's history. Others are pieces of much smaller asteroids that preserve the primordial dust from which Earth and other planets first formed. A rare few come from the Moon and Mars. Many dust-sized micrometeorites may come from comets. The chance encounters of meteorites with Earth provide us with an extraordinary look at distant worlds and give us a chance to discover something about the processes that gave birth to our world and the larger solar system.

Nakhla meteorite, fell near Nakhla al Baharia, close to Alexandria, Egypt, in 1911, about 1 billion years old. NMNH

This meteorite—an igneous rock composed of crystals of pyroxene, olivine, and traces of feldspar—came from Mars. The rock formed there more than 1 billion years ago. It is very young in comparison to most meteorites.

Geologists have discovered gas in the meteorite that closely matches the Martian atmosphere, which had already been analyzed by the Viking spacecraft. The gas was trapped in the rock when a giant asteroid hit Mars and sent it hurtling toward Earth.

Canyon Diablo meteorite, found just west of Canyon Diablo near Meteor Crater, Arizona in 1897, about 4.5 billion years old. NMNH

This meteorite is fragment of a large asteroid long ago destroyed by a colossal impact in Arizona about 50,000 years ago. The meteorite created a bowl–shaped hole 1,200 meters (0.75 miles) across and 200 meters (650 feet) deep, known as Meteor Crater. The meteor was so large—estimated at 30 meters (100 feet) in diameter—that it was not appreciably slowed by its passage through Earth's atmosphere.

About 1930, Meteor Crater became the first crater generally accepted by scientists to be the product of meteoritic impact. It is one of the best studied in the world. Although most of the meteorite vaporized at impact, some 20,000 fragments, weighing more than 30 tons altogether, have been recovered. This specimen is one of the few large masses of the original meteorite yet discovered. Signs showing that it flew independently through the atmosphere indicate that it probably separated from the main mass before impact. It was discovered near Canyon Diablo, 10 miles northwest of Meteor Crater.

Discovering Life on a Living Planet

MOLLUSKS

Scientists have identified, analyzed, and classified more than 1 million different species of animals. We continue to discover new species every year as we penetrate further into the secrets contained in Nature's vast book. The ultimate goals of taxonomy—the science of classifying animal species—are to reveal the relationships among animals and to illuminate the history of life on our planet. Taxonomy provides us with the foundation of our biological knowledge and permits us to understand better our own place in relation to other living creatures. As one noted zoologist observed, "taxonomy is at the same time the most elementary and the most inclusive part of zoology."

Since its beginning, the Smithsonian has been a center of taxonomic research. The Institution's vast collections contain more than 60 million specimens of species that reflect the biodiversity of our world. Viewed as a whole or in part, the Smithsonian's collections give us a sense of wonder at the complexity, beauty, order, and mystery of the natural world.

Cuban land snails *(Polymita picta)*, 3 specimens. NMNH

Marine shell, imperial delphinus *(Angaria imperialis)*. NMNH

The second largest phylum after arthropods, Mollusca encompasses more than 70,000 species, including land snails, freshwater snails and clams, marine snails, clams, squids, and octopuses. The phylum is so large that taxonomists are well aware that they have not yet discovered and described every mollusk species. The primary characteristic of mollusks is the hard shell protecting their soft bodies. Even squids, octopuses, and land and sea slugs retain evolutionary fragments of internal shells, even though they usually lack external shells.

The Smithsonian's Mollusk Collection contains more than 15 million specimens representing the diversity of the phylum. Scientists look beyond the beauty of mollusk shells in order to discover how these animals live and adapt to their surroundings. One of the most beautiful— and deadly—mollusk families is the Conidae, a family of marine snails with cone-shaped shells. These mollusks possess a harpoon-shaped hollow tooth containing a potent neurotoxin that paralyzes their prey. The venom can kill humans as well as fish, the primary prey of cones.

Marine shell, rose branch murex *(Chicoreus palmarosae)*. NMNH

Marine shells, true heart cockles *(Corculum cardissa)*, two specimens. NMNH

FROM LEFT: Marine shell, golden cowrie *(Cypraea aurantium)*; marine shell, eyed cowrie *(Cypraea argus)*. NMNH

Marine shell, trumpet triton *(Charonia tritonis).*
NMNH

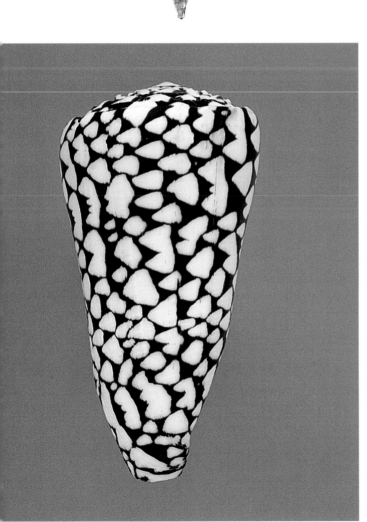

Marine shell, geography
cone *(Conus geographus).*
NMNH

Marine shell, marble cone
(Conus marmoreus).
NMNH

Marine shell, Yoka star
turban *(Guildfordia yoka)*.
NMNH

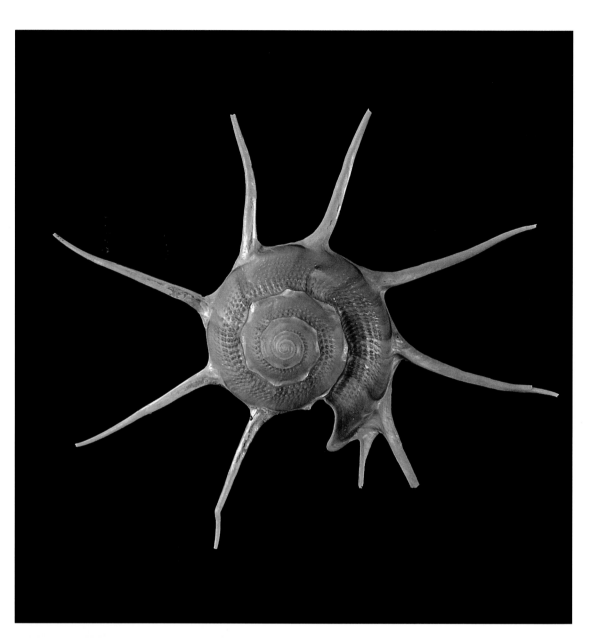

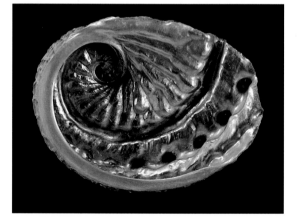

Marine shell, staircase
abalone *(Haliotis scalaris)*,
two views. NMNH

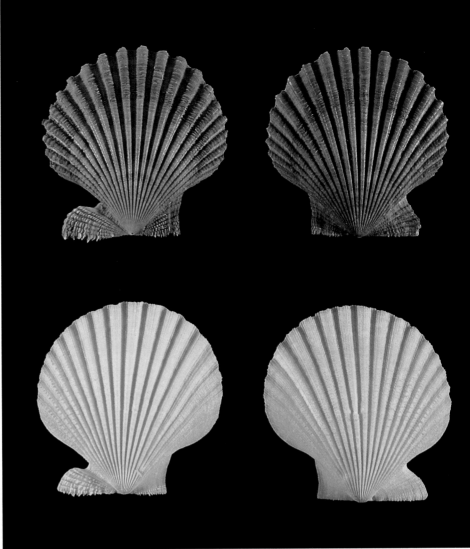

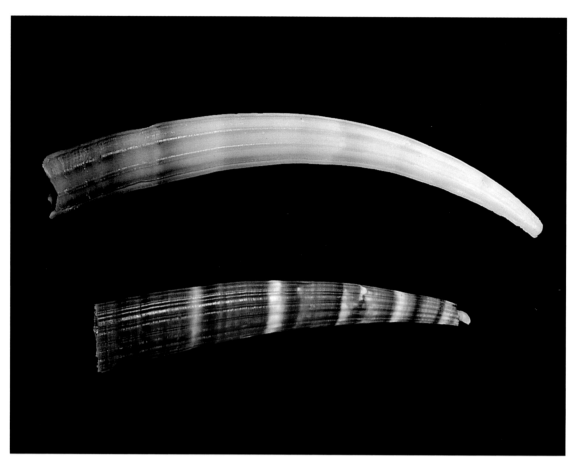

FROM TOP: Marine shell,
elephant tusk *(Dentalium
elephantinum)*; marine
shell, Formosan tusk
*(Pictodentalivin
formosum)*. NMNH

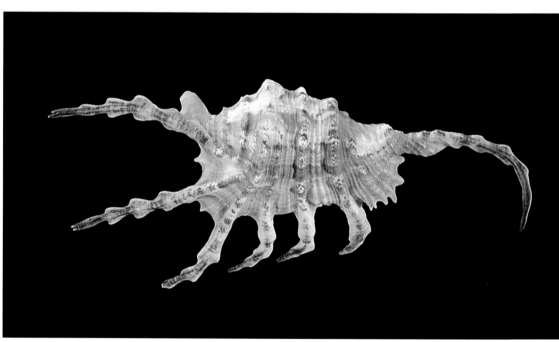

Marine shell, false Scorpio
conch *(Lambis robusta)*.
NMNH

Discovering the Underwater World

Like an ancient city whose foundations rest on ruins, a reef is built on its own refuse and remains. Far more than just a rigid framework of stony skeletons, a reef is mostly detritus and sediment, produced and held in place by various reef residents. By studying reefs, we can learn not only about the biodiversity of underwater life but also about the interdependence of animals within an ecosystem and the events that affected the formation of reefs.

Coral reefs thrive in sites with clear, shallow water and stable, warm temperatures. Soft-bodied animals called polyps provide the foundation of coral reefs with the calcium-rich skeletons produced by the outer layer of their skins. It takes billions of polyps centuries to build a reef that can provide shelter for a vast array of other animals. In the favorable conditions provided by reefs, competition for living space becomes keen. Like most city dwellers, reef inhabitants solve the urban space problem by building upward and by moving farther out. As a reef grows higher, it creates stacked, packed neighborhoods, each with characteristic residents. Around the reef live fishes and other suburbanites, including sea fans (a kind of octocoral) as well as starfish and sea urchins, both members of the phylum Echinodermata.

Sun starfish *(Heliaster helianthus)*. NMNH

Sea urchin *(Hetero-centrotus trigonarius)*. NMNH

Reef coral *(Pectinia alci-cornis)*. NMNH

Purple sea fan *(Gorgona ventalina)* and yellow sea fan *(Gorgona flabellum)*. NMNH

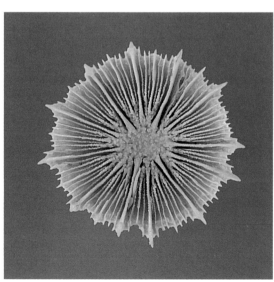

Deep-water coral *(Stephanocyathus diadema)*, two views. NMNH

OPPOSITE: Basket starfish *(Gorgonocephalus caryi)*. NMNH

Art and Scientific Discovery

John James Audubon, portrait by an unknown artist after an 1841 original by John Woodhouse Audubon, the naturalist's son, oil on canvas. NPG

In his youth, John James Audubon (1785–1851) had been fascinated with observing and drawing birds, but during his early adulthood, he put aside those interests to become a Kentucky storekeeper. In 1820 his business failed, and Audubon began traveling the frontier, making sketches of birds in their habitats. By 1826 he was in England overseeing the publication of these drawings in a series of giant folios entitled *The Birds of America.* It was twelve years before the folios were completed. With the appearance of the first in the late 1820s, French naturalist Georges Cuvier declared that Audubon was creating "the most magnificent monument that art had yet raised to science."

Audubon's efforts to stir interest in his work were remarkably successful. Through his naturalistic renderings of birds and quadrupeds in their habitats, he acquainted people throughout the United States and Europe with the beauty and diversity of American wildlife. His audiences, past and present, not only can appreciate the beauty of his artistic technique but also can participate in the scientist's keen observation of living creatures when viewing his work.

Audubon found that he could draw greater public attention by dressing like a woodsman. When his son painted the original version of this portrait, he may have been motivated by the thought that this was how the public wanted to see his father.

Audubon has inspired generations of Americans to study and appreciate their natural surroundings and the animal life in them. For students, scientists, and the general public in the 19th century, Audubon's works formed the basis of their knowledge of North American fauna.

A naturalized U.S. citizen born in the French colony of St. Domingue (later Haiti) and raised in France, Audubon became famous for his dramatic and beautiful watercolor drawings of the birds of North America. An artist and self-taught naturalist, he liked to draw birds in their natural habitats, capturing their images in poses suggestive of sudden movement. This style was notably different from the stiff poses found in earlier guides to birds. Despite being criticized for the lack of scientific accuracy in his drawings and written descriptions, Audubon became one of the most influential naturalists of all time.

The Birds of America, written with his friend John Bachman (1790–1874), a South Carolina clergyman and naturalist, was first published in a very large (double elephant) folio edition in 1827–38. It was republished a number of times and in a number of sizes in Audubon's lifetime, including the smaller octavo-size edition on display here.

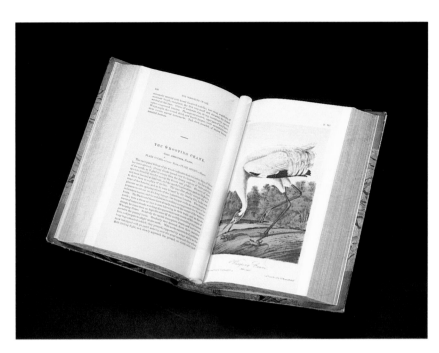

The Birds of North America, volume 5, by John James Audubon and John Bachman, 1839. SIL

The Quadrupeds of North America, volume 2, by John James Audubon and John Bachman, 1854. SIL

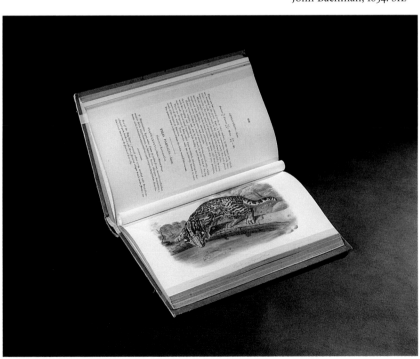

Audubon began this illustrated guide to the four-footed animals of North America in collaboration with John Bachman. Audubon, who did not live to see the work completed, contributed about half the drawings and some anecdotal observations. His sons, John Woodhouse and Victor Gifford Audubon, drew many of the animals and the background settings with the assistance of several other artists. Bachman was responsible for the scientific content and edited the entire work.

The collaborators sought to depict animals in realistic landscapes, although at that time many species of animals in North America were only rarely seen and little had been discovered about their ways of life. In some cases, Audubon and Bachman had to rely on second-hand descriptions or on stuffed specimens as models for animals included in the book.

Originally published in a very large (double elephant) folio edition under the title *Viviparous Quadrupeds of North America,* this volume is from a later, smaller-sized edition that carries the inscription to "Greene Smith, from his father, May, 1858."

INSECTS

BEETLES

Insects won't inherit the earth—they own it now.

—THOMAS EISNER, entomologist

Of the more than 1 million animal species we have identified, about 85 percent are insects. For every person on the planet, there are approximately 200 million insects. Insects are the most diversified and successful of all animals. They are crucial to every terrestrial ecosystem on the planet. Many dispose of dead animal and plant matter, as well as animal waste. Some are major plant eaters that process and return nutrients to the soil. Others pollinate flowers and are vital to plant reproduction and crop cultivation. Still others provide us with products like silk, honey, beeswax, and even shellac. Our survival, indeed the survival of all other animals and plants, depends upon the work of insects.

Insects are members of the phylum Arthropoda, which also includes spiders, millipedes, centipedes, and crustaceans. Insects lack backbones, but possess external skeletons made of chitin and have six jointed legs. Their bodies are divided into three segments—head, thorax, and abdomen. Beyond these characteristics, their physical attributes are extraordinarily varied. On the basis of their special characteristics, we classify insects into thirty-three major orders, each of which contains thousands of species.

The insect collection in the Smithsonian contains roughly 30 million specimens. It is one of the richest in the world, the product of centuries of collection, classification, and research.

Buprestid beetle (*Megaloxantha bicolor,* Family Buprestidae).

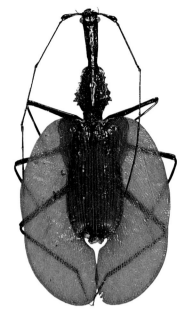

Violin beetle (*Mormolyce* sp., Family Carabidae).

Unicorn beetle (*Dynastes hercules,* Family Scarabaeidae).

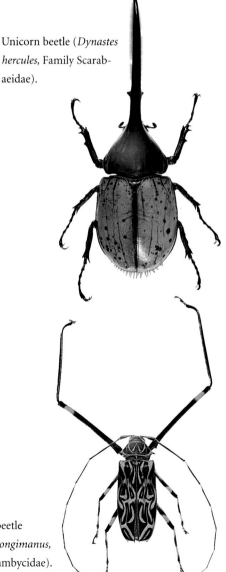

Harlequin beetle (*Acrocinus longimanus,* Family Cerambycidae).

Australian weevil (*Pachyrrhynchus smaragdinus,* Family Curculionidae).

Red weevil (*Rhyncophorus cruentatus,* Family Curculionidae).

Goliath beetle (*Goliathus goliatus*, Family Scarabaeidae).

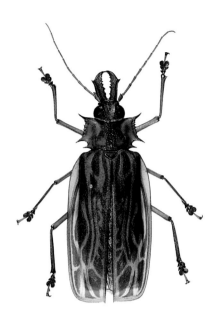

Long-horned beetle (*Macrodontia cervicornis*, Family Cerambycidae).

Plusiotis leaf chafer beetle (*Plusiotis gloriosa*, Family Scarabaeidae).

Spotted chafer beetle (*Stephanorrhina guttata*, Family Scarabaeidae).

Green Brazilian weevil (*Lamprocyphus* sp., Family Curculionidae).

We have identified more than 300,000 beetle species, and we know that more than a million exist. They comprise the largest group of insects, accounting for about two-fifths of all known species.

Beetles usually possess a thickened pair of forewings that cover a membranous set of hindwings. Most fly, but a few do not. Beetles' feeding habits range from predation to parasitism to dung feeding. Their sensory organs, including their eyes, are concentrated on their heads, but they also have vibration-sensitive hairs covering their bodies. Beetles undergo complete metamorphosis—from egg to larva to pupa to adult. The species have evolved different characteristics

to cope with different environments. Some, for example, have long skinny legs evolved for scuttling quickly after their prey. Others have broad, notched legs adapted for digging.

The weevils are an important subgroup within the beetle order, primarily because of their effect on humans. Many feed on the seeds, flowers, and leaves of human crops. The boll weevil, with its taste for cotton fiber, ravaged southern crops early in the 20th century. The biscuit weevil, with its appetite for hard tack and flour, used to plague sailors. All NMNH

Jewel weevil (*Pachyrrhynchus* sp., Family Curculionidae).

Pink weevil (*Exophthalmus vittatus*, Family Curculionidae).

Lined scarab beetle (*Dicronorrhina derbyana*, Family Scarabaeidae).

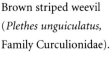

Brown striped weevil (*Plethes unguiculatus*, Family Curculionidae).

Orange weevil (*Agalmatus* sp., Family Curculionidae).

Butterflies and Moths

Between 150,000 and 200,000 known species of the order *Lepidoptera* ("scale-wing") live wherever there is vegetation. Adult butterflies and moths usually have wings with overlapping scales covering transparent membranes. When we handle butterflies and moths, the "dust" that comes off in our hands is composed of these minute scales.

The magnificent patterns and colors that these insects exhibit result either from pigments in the scales or from their physical structure. The scales of some species, like morpho butterflies, refract bands of color when light hits them, producing an intensely iridescent effect. While for us their wing colors are the source of delight, for butterflies and moths their hues serve very practical purposes, including camouflage and sexual self-advertisement. Certain patterns of coloration also warn off predators.

The distinction between butterflies and moths is more artificial than real, although most moths are active at night and most butterflies flutter in the sunlight, showing off their brilliant hues. All NMNH

Sunset moth (*Chrysiridia ripheus,* Family Uraniidae), Madagascar.

Glassywing butterfly (*Idea* sp., Family Nymphalidae), Phillippines.

CLOCKWISE FROM TOP LEFT: Moon moth (*Argema mittrei,* Family Saturniidae), Uganda; Atlas moth (*Attacus* sp., Family Saturniidae), India; owl butterfly (*Caligo* sp., Family Nymphalidae), Brazil; Brahmeid moth (*Brahmaea wallichii,* Family Brahmaeidae), India.

Swallowtail butterfly
(*Papilio hesperus*, Family
Papilionidae), Uganda.

Brazilian blue morpho
butterfly (*Morpho* sp.,
Family Nymphalidae).

Birdwing butterfly
(*Ornithoptera* sp., Family
Papilionidae), Malaysia.

Brush-footed butterfly
(*Charaxes* sp., Family
Nymphalidae), Sierra
Leone.

Monarch butterfly
(*Danaus plexippus*, Family
Danaidae), United States.

Venezuelan blue morpho
butterfly (*Morpho* sp.,
Family Nymphalidae).

The Active Pursuit of Discovery

Our desire to decipher the mysteries in Nature's book has inspired countless expeditions to record information and retrieve specimens for study. Throughout human history, men and women have actively sought to acquire greater knowledge of the world around them. Their discoveries have ultimately led to new theories about the nature of the physical universe and the life our planet contains.

Since the beginning of the 20th century, new technologies have enabled us to expand the boundaries of exploration and increased our thirst for new knowledge. Our exploration of space has barely begun. Now, with instruments like the Hubble telescope orbiting the earth, we can explore ever further into distant galaxies and even, in a sense, travel back in time to learn about the origins of the universe. We continue to invent new methods and means for reading the book of Nature.

AMERICAN LAND AND SEA EXPEDITIONS

After the American Revolution, the United States government sponsored numerous land and sea expeditions. On these journeys, American explorers and scientists recorded their observations and collected specimens for future study. Many of the objects they collected became among the first objects housed in the new United States National Museum, now the Smithsonian Institution.

Compass and case carried by William Clark during the expedition by Lewis and Clark to the Pacific coast, 1804. NMAH

In 1803, President Thomas Jefferson arranged the purchase of the Louisiana territory from France and nearly doubled the size of the United States. Most Americans living in the east knew little about this enormous tract of land. One of the first expeditions into the area was the journey by Captains Meriwether Lewis and William Clark into the northwestern part of the territory. Specifically charged by President Jefferson, they kept detailed records of the wildlife and geological features they encountered on the journey.

William Clark carried this compass during the expedition. The paper dial is marked "T. Whitney Philada." to identify its maker and is set in a mahogany box bound in brass. The leather case for the box has straps that allow it to be fastened to a belt.

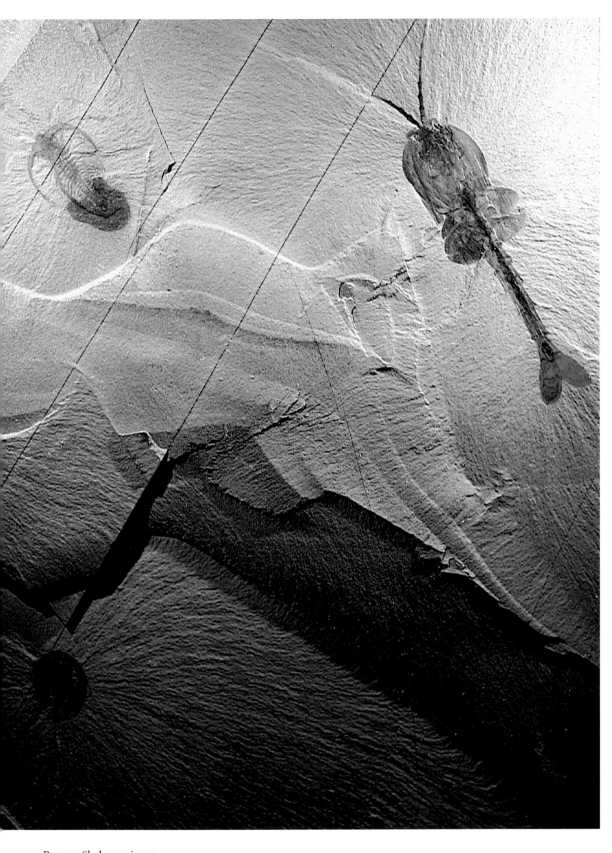

Burgess Shale specimen
with fossil arthropods
(*Marrella splendens,
Waptia fieldensis,
Burgessia bella*), Middle
Cambrian period, about
520 million years old.
NMNH

In 1909 the Smithsonian's
fourth Secretary, geolo-
gist Charles D. Walcott,
discovered the Burgess
Shale deposit in British
Columbia. It provided
the first evidence of the
early diversity of soft-
bodied organisms, some
of which are so unique
that all efforts to link
them with other known
animals have been unsuc-
cessful. About 40 percent
of the species preserved
in the Burgess Shale have
not been found anywhere
else.

The deposit formed
when masses of mud and
silt periodically fell to the
base of an underwater
cliff during avalanches
and formed clouds of fine
particles that trapped living animals and plants.
The life-choking cloud
settled, burying the
organisms in an environ-
ment free of scavengers.
In this way, the deposit
preserved the organisms'
delicate tissues in remarkable detail.

This discovery pro-
vides us with an extraor-
dinary glimpse into the
life of ancient seas, and it
proves that marine ani-
mals without hard shells
or skeletons were numer-
ous during the Cambrian
period. More important,
the specimens hint at the
true variety of Cambrian
animals and remind us
that life in the past was far
more diverse than most
fossil records indicate.

The Wilkes Expedition

The United States Exploring Expedition of 1838–42 led by Lieutenant Charles Wilkes (1798–1877) was the first international scientific survey sponsored by the U.S. government and the first to employ professional scientists. The scientists surveyed 300 islands, drafted 200 maps and charts, mapped 800 miles of the Oregon coast, and confirmed the existence of Antarctica as a continent. They also collected vast numbers of natural specimens and artifacts.

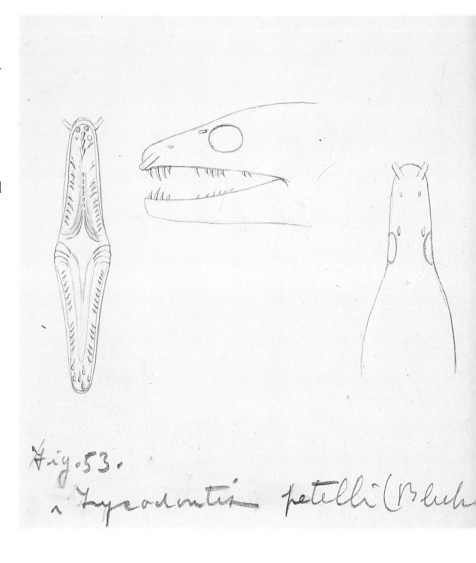

Drawing from the Wilkes Expedition, 1838–42. SA

Accompanying the Wilkes Expedition were nine civilian scientists. The expedition was the first peacetime scientific mission carried out jointly by naval personnel and civilians. It also represented an important step in the United States' evolution into an international scientific power. Its crew amassed a huge natural history collection from all over the world.

The need for a museum to house this collection, as well as others, led to a provision for a museum in the founding legislation for the Smithsonian. In 1858 the collections were transferred to the Smithsonian, establishing the United States National Museum and the foundation for the largest museum complex in the world.

This illustration of *Lysodontis stellatia,* a sea eel, was probably drawn aboard ship by one of the artists, Alfred T. Agate or Joseph Drayton, for the naturalists, Titian Ramsey Peale and Charles Pickering.

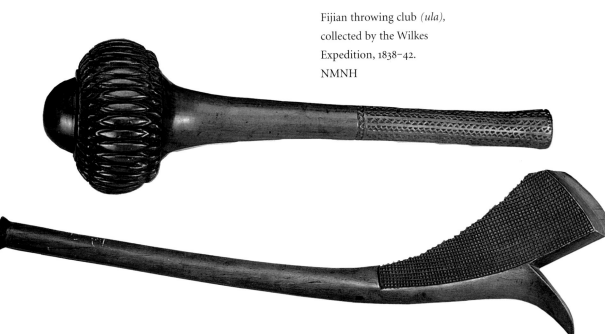

Fijian throwing club *(ula),* collected by the Wilkes Expedition, 1838–42. NMNH

During the journey, the Wilkes Expedition stopped on the island of Fiji. The Smithsonian Institution currently holds more than 1,200 objects acquired by the expedition that document various aspects of Fijian cultural life. These clubs were used either in warfare or for ceremonial performances.

Fijian club *(sali),* collected by the Wilkes Expedition, 1838–42. NMNH

Charles Wilkes published a five-volume narrative account of the United States Exploring Expedition in 1844. He spent the next seventeen years supervising the publication of another fifteen volumes and nine atlases of scientific studies on the specimens and information that his crew had collected.

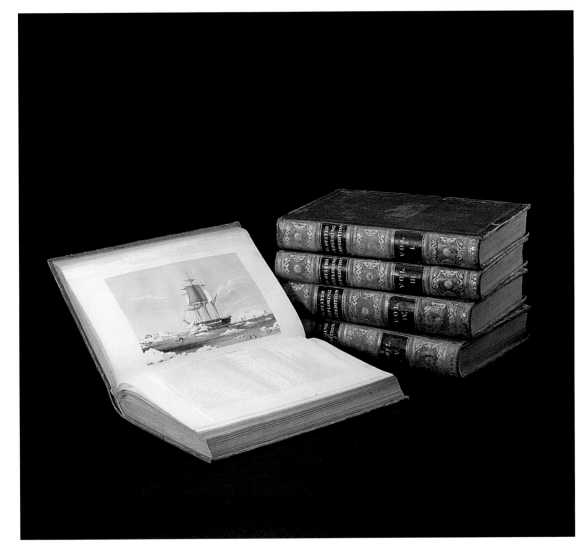

1849 edition of the *Narrative of the United States Exploring Expedition,* volume 1, by Charles Wilkes, first published in 1844. SIL

Further, Higher, Faster

Leonardo da Vinci and other inventors longed to fly and created countless designs of flying machines. People flew kites, hot air balloons, and gliders, which became increasingly popular in the late 19th century. But powered human flight remained an elusive goal until the invention of the internal combustion engine.

Wilbur and Orville Wright applied that new technology to the problem of powered flight. The brothers initiated the age of modern aviation with their 12-second flight at Kitty Hawk, North Carolina on December 17, 1903. The advent of the airplane forever changed transportation,

commerce, and warfare, and greatly extended our ability to explore the world.

Soon after the Wright brothers' success, barnstormers, aviators, and test pilots took to the skies. With every passing year, records were set and broken. Flights across oceans, continents, and through the sound barrier made the reputations of aviation heroes like Cal Rogers, Amelia Earhart, Charles Lindbergh, and Chuck Yeager. The Smithsonian's aeronautical collections record the history of technological development and pay tribute to the people who dreamed and dared to fly.

Charles A. Lindbergh won this check for his completion of the first nonstop flight from New York City to Paris on May 20–21, 1927. Raymond Orteig, a New York hotel owner born in France, had offered a prize of $25,000 to encourage a transatlantic flight between New York and Paris.

Lindbergh's solo flight aboard the Ryan NYP *Spirit of St. Louis,* together with his modest but heroic persona, captured public imagination in the United States and abroad. The United States Congress awarded him the Medal of Honor and the first Distinguished Flying Cross. The governments of France, Great Britain, Belgium, Spain, and Canada, among others, awarded him medals and commemorative plaques. Lindbergh's flight took on a mythic quality, symbolizing the human capacity to overcome physical barriers.

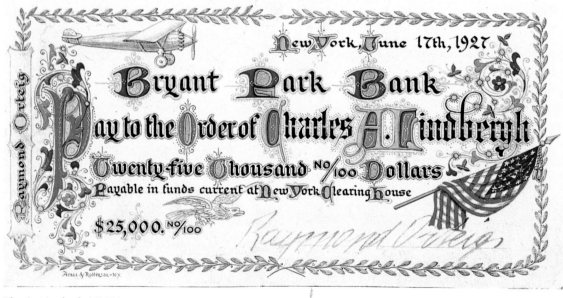

The Orteig check. NASM

OPPOSITE: Amelia Earhart's flight suit. NPM

Born in Atchison, Kansas, in 1898, Amelia Earhart became the first woman to cross the Atlantic by air in 1928. Although the crew on that flight did not permit her to pilot the plane, she soon made her independent mark on aviation history by flying solo across the Atlantic in 1932. She departed from Canada on May 20—five years to the day after Charles Lindbergh's solo flight across the Atlantic. She landed her red Lockheed Vega in James Gallagher's pasture near Londonderry, Ireland, on May 21.

After her Atlantic crossing. Earhart made other record-breaking long-distance flights, including a 1935 flight from Honolulu to Oakland, California. In 1937 she tried to become the first woman pilot to fly around the world. During the segment of her journey between New Guinea and Howland Island in the Pacific, her plane vanished. Earhart's fate remains the source of much speculation.

Earhart's flannel-lined leather flying suit provided her with extra warmth. Insulated flying suits were essential for long-distance flights. Early airplanes offered scant protection from the elements, especially the icy cold at 20,000 feet (6,096 meters).

Amelia Earhart cover from 1932 transatlantic flight. NPM

During Amelia Earhart's solo flight across the Atlantic on May 20–21, 1932, she carried fifty prenumbered covers, of which this is number 15. She had the covers postmarked at Londonderry on May 23 to prove her arrival.

Although New York City was planning a huge reception to welcome Earhart home, she telegraphed Mayor James Walker requesting that the ceremonies be canceled. Since the country was in the midst of the Great Depression, she suggested, the money would be better spent on the needs of the unemployed. Earhart's homecoming nonetheless drew thousands of admirers who lined Broadway and showered her with ticker-tape.

Captain Charles E. (Chuck) Yeager wore this standard United States Air Force issue leather jacket when he piloted the Bell X-1 and became the first man to fly faster than the speed of sound on October 14, 1947. The Bell X-1 reached a speed of 700 miles (1,127 kilometers) per hour––Mach 1.06––at an altitude of 43,000 feet (13,000 meters).

The Bell X-1 was launched at an altitude of 23,000 feet (7,000 meters) from the bomb bay of a Boeing B-29 and used its rocket engine to climb to its test altitude. It flew seventy-eight times, and on March 26, 1948, it attained a speed of 957 miles (1,540 kilometers) per hour––Mach 1.45––at an altitude of 71,900 feet

(21,900 meters), the highest velocity and altitude ever reached by a manned airplane until that time. Yeager named the plane "Glamorous Glennis" in tribute to his wife.

Chuck Yeager's jacket. NASM

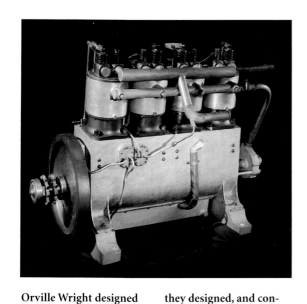

Wright Brothers engine.
NASM

Orville Wright designed this 35-horsepower, 4-cylinder vertical aircraft engine in 1906. The Wrights produced greater numbers of this engine model than any other

The Vin Fiz aircraft.
NASM

they designed, and continued its production until about 1912. The U.S. Army and several European countries used them for aerial demonstrations—a factor cru-

cial to the Wright brothers' success. An engine of this type powered the Wright EX "Vin Fiz," the first aircraft to make a U.S. transcontinental flight in 1911.

This engine was the keepsake of Orville Wright for many years. He gave it to his close friend, Jim Jacobs, who had been the mechanic with the original Wright Brothers Company.

BELOW: The Wright brothers inaugurated the aerial age with the first successful powered airplane flight at Kitty Hawk, North Carolina, on December 17, 1903. By 1905 they had transformed their original underpowered and unstable flying machine into a practical airplane. Within five years they had formed a company to manufacture and sell aircraft.

Calbraith Perry Rodgers, a descendent of Commodore Matthew Perry, piloted this Wright EX wood-and-fabric biplane called the "Vin Fiz" on the first United States transcontinental flight in 1911. The Armour

Packing Company, makers of the Vin Fiz grape soda, sponsored the flight.

Rodgers was thirty-two years old and had fewer than 60 hours of flying experience when he embarked on his transcontinental adventure. He held his course by following railway lines and made 70 stops during his 84-day flight, often crash landing. The airplane had to be entirely rebuilt four times during his 4,321-mile (6,954-kilometer) odyssey. Rodgers died in the crash of another airplane during an air show only four months after completing his flight in the Vin Fiz.

Reaching beyond the Earth

Between 1903 and 1961 Americans moved from attaining a 12-second powered flight on the beaches of Kitty Hawk to sending a human being into outer space. In the 1950s the United States began probing beyond the earth's atmosphere with satellites and unmanned vehicles. Beginning in 1961, with Alan Shepard's flight aboard *Freedom 7,* Americans expanded their reach into space through the manned flights of the Mercury, Gemini, and Apollo programs. Monumental achievements in space flight punctuated the 1960s. The decade culminated with two Americans landing on the moon on July 20, 1969.

The expeditions and discoveries on our own planet have ultimately allowed us to venture out beyond our world in the pursuit of knowledge. From the vantage point of space, we continue to learn more about our own planet and the universe. The Smithsonian's aerospace collections document the progress of the space program and commemorate the men and women who have transformed our dream to reach beyond the earth into a reality.

Vanguard I satellite.
NASM

On July 29, 1955, President Dwight D. Eisenhower announced that the United States would launch a small, unmanned satellite into orbit around the earth. He initiated Project Vanguard to accomplish this goal during the planned International Geophysical Year (August 1957–December 1958).

Following the successful Soviet launches of Sputnik I on October 4 and Sputnik II on November 11, 1957, the American government and public placed great pressure on the Vanguard team to launch an American satellite. On December 6, 1957, a Vanguard rocket carrying a satellite exploded on the launch pad. On January 31, 1958, the U.S. Army team led by Wernher von Braun used a Jupiter C rocket to put Explorer I into orbit. On March 15, 1958, Vanguard I became America's second satellite in space.

This satellite served as the backup to the Vanguard I satellite. Its payload is identical in all aspects to those of the satellites launched on December 6, 1957, and March 15, 1958.

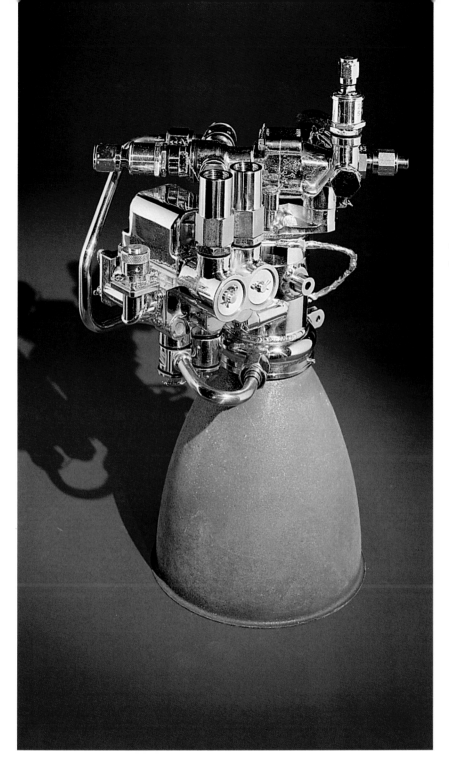

Surveyor vernier rocket engine. NASM

Surveyor lunar probes, launched during the late 1960s, were the United States' first spacecraft to soft-land on the moon. The probes' vernier engines were critical to these missions because they provided small, precise bursts of power for midcourse correction maneuvers and attitude (position) controls. This allowed the probes to land exactly as planned on the moon. The verniers had to work perfectly every time and were made to withstand the extreme temperatures of outer space. They also had to provide adjustable amounts of thrust in order to start and stop as needed.

Thiokol Chemical Corporation made the verniers. Each lunar probe had three engines—one for each of its landing legs. Each vernier gave 30–104 pounds of thrust (13.6–47 kilograms) but weighed only 5.9 pounds (2.7 kilograms), minus the liquid fuel tankage. To reflect hazardous radiation, highly polished gold plate 0.0001–inch (0.00254–millimeter) thick coated parts of the engines. The nozzle—the green section of this artifact—had a highly heat-resistant ceramic coating. Electric command signals controlled the throttle and the on-off valves.

Of the five lunar surveyors launched between 1966 and 1968, all of the vernier engines worked except one. The Surveyor program produced invaluable pictures and data for the Apollo manned lunar landing program.

On May 5, 1961, Alan Shepard became the first American in space. Enclosed in this Mercury spacecraft, the *Freedom 7*, Shepard rode atop a Redstone rocket to an altitude of 116 miles (187 kilometers) and a maximum speed of 5,180 miles (8336 kilometers) per hour. The flight of *Freedom 7* lasted 15 minutes, 22 seconds, and ended in the Atlantic Ocean, just over 300 miles (483 kilometers) from the launch pad at Cape Canaveral, Florida.

About three weeks before the launch of *Freedom 7*, Soviet cosmonaut Yuri Gagarin became the first man in space and the first to orbit the earth. Shepard's flight marked America's first step in what became an extended effort by the United States to match and exceed Soviet accomplishments in space. Three weeks after the flight of *Freedom 7*, President John F. Kennedy proposed to Congress that the United States commit itself to a manned lunar landing before the end of the decade.

The Mercury spacecraft is approximately 9 feet (2.7 meters) high and 6 feet (1.8 meters) in diameter at its base. Two parachutes fit in the cylindrical upper section of the craft. The craft reentered the atmosphere bottom end down. The shield on the bottom protected the astronaut and the rest of the spacecraft from the tremendous heat generated as the spacecraft plunged back through the atmosphere.

Freedom 7 Mercury spacecraft. NASM

BELOW: Neil Armstrong, Edwin "Buzz" Aldrin, and Michael Collins began their journey to the moon on the morning of July 16, 1969, in the command module *Columbia* atop a Saturn V rocket. They achieved lunar orbit on July 20 and flew an average of 60 miles above the moon's surface. Armstrong and Aldrin then boarded the lunar landing module *Eagle*, and they became the first astronauts to land on the moon 4 days, 6 hours, 45 minutes, and 47 seconds after their flight began. In 1971 Collins became the first director of the Smithsonian's National Air and Space Museum.

The crew of Apollo 11 carried these lunar maps on their mission to the moon in July 1969. The United States Army Topographic Command had prepared the maps specifically for the first lunar landing.

The Apollo 14 command
module, *Kitty Hawk*.
NASM

Apollo 11 lunar maps

President John F. Kennedy's dream to land a man on the moon inspired the Apollo missions. The third lunar mission, Apollo 14, resumed manned exploration of the moon nine months after disaster aborted the Apollo 13 flight. Apollo 14 was launched on January 31, 1971, atop a Saturn V rocket from complex 39A at the Kennedy Space Center. Alan Shepard—who ten years earlier had become the first American in space—commanded the mission. Stuart Roosa was the pilot of the command module *Kitty Hawk,* and Edgar Mitchell, pilot of the lunar module *Antares.*

The Saturn rocket carried the *Kitty Hawk* and the *Antares* beyond the earth's atmosphere. Following their entry into lunar orbit, Shepard and Mitchell climbed into *Antares,* separated from the command module, and landed in the Fra Mauro region of the moon.

Lunar rover. NASM

This lunar roving vehicle vibration testing unit is almost identical to the rovers that American astronauts used during the Apollo 15, 16, and 17 lunar missions. The astronauts trained with this rover before their flights in order to test the levels of vibration they were likely to experience.

The electric-powered Lunar Roving Vehicles (LRVs) permitted astronauts to explore much larger areas of the moon's surface than they could have on foot. About the size of a golf cart, the rover had four .25-horsepower electric motors, one built into each wheel. Two 36-volt electric batteries powered the vehicle, the second acting as a fail-safe backup. Because both the front and rear wheels could be used to steer, the LRV could turn in a circle as tight as 10 feet (3 meters) in diameter.

Lunar rovers traveled to the moon in the lower "descent" stage of the lunar module. The wheels, seats, and antenna all folded inward, making a compact package. No provisions were made to return the rovers to Earth. Considered much more valuable, and a better use of available space, were the samples of lunar soil and rocks collected with the help of the rovers.

Walking and working in space posed tremendous technical challenges. Apollo spacesuits provided a lightweight, reliable, complete life-support system that could be easily stored and donned. The outer layer consisted of an integrated thermal protection assembly that guarded against micrometeor impact, fire, and extreme temperatures ranging from +250 degrees Fahrenheit in the sunlight to -250 degrees Fahrenheit in shadow.

The inner suit consisted of twenty-one layers of material, including a comfort liner made of Nomex (high-temperature-resistant nylon), a neoprine-coated nylon bladder to hold pressurized air, and an outer nylon restraint structure. Specially designed joints provided the flexibility needed to accommodate body movements.

Underneath the suit, the astronaut wore a cooling garment consisting of a layer of nylon spandex with a network of tubing that carried cool water over his body in order to prevent sweating and dehydration. A ventilation system provided oxygen, removed carbon dioxide and moisture, and controlled total body pressure.

The space suit, combined with the life support system, weighed about 180 pounds (81.6 kilograms) on earth or approximately 30 pounds (13.6 kilograms) in reduced lunar gravity.

Commander David Scott wore this spacesuit on the Apollo 15 lunar mission launched on July 26, 1971.

Apollo 15 space suit.
NASM

Imagining

The ability to imagine—to reach beyond what is known—lies at the heart of human creativity. Our imagination allows us to solve practical problems, to address challenges, and to create works of art that delight and engage us.

The Smithsonian's art museums collect, preserve, and display thousands of objects that celebrate human imagination. They carry out research into art history and present outreach programs that teach us about our aesthetic heritage and enrich our cultural life. Art works have been an important part of the Institution's collections since its founding in 1846.

The Institution's museums contain treasures from a wide range of places and time periods. The artists who created the pieces shown here worked within the conventions alive in their cultures. But they also reshaped and reached beyond established traditions in order to communicate their ideas.

Detail of *Mist in Kanab Canyon* by Thomas Moran

Creating an American Vision

As a group, these paintings illustrate the inspiration of the American experience as well as an indebtedness to classical and European artistic conventions. The two sculptures created by European artists exemplify some of the stylistic influences that have inspired American artists.

Draped Reclining Figure, 1952–53, by Henry Moore, bronze. HMSG

Henry Moore (1898–1986) began his career carving directly in wood and stone. After World War II, he largely abandoned this technique in order to create large-scale outdoor pieces. He began making plaster and clay models that were better suited than his earlier works for enlargement and reproduction in bronze. In these sculptures, Moore fused Abstraction with the conventions evident in monumental pieces from earlier periods to achieve a timeless quality of his own. He found inspiration in the art of earlier traditions, ranging from ancient Greece to pre-Columbian America.

Moore merged the traditional subject matter of the human figure with a Surrealist emphasis on flowing, curving forms inspired by the shapes of living organisms. He envisioned *Draped Reclining Figure* in 1951, when he traveled to Greece and studied the robed figures sculpted by classical artists during the 5th and 4th centuries B.C.

The South Ledges, Appledore, by Childe Hassam, 1913, oil on canvas. NMAA

One of America's foremost impressionists, **Childe Hassam (1859–1935) found much of his inspiration on the Isles of Shoals off the coast of New Hampshire, where an estate named Appledore was located. There, Celia Laighton Thaxter (1835–94), an essayist and poet, welcomed artists, writers, and musicians to sum-**mer salons where they **could enjoy her extensive gardens and the wild beauty of the craggy New England coast. Hassam thrived at Appledore. Many of his paintings either depicted the Isles or were created there. He painted this work during his last summer at the retreat.**

In *The South Ledges, Appledore,* Hassam's painting technique and **pure colors recall Monet's *Belle Isle* paintings. Hassam would become quite annoyed whenever people compared his work with that of the French Impressionist. But he must have found Impressionism a most effective means of conveying the beauty of the rocky, seaweed-laden shoreline emptying into** the vibrant, foaming, sunlit ocean of this painting.

Mist in Kanab Canyon, by Thomas Moran, 1882, oil on canvas. NMAA

Like all of Thomas Moran's (1837–1927) celebrated western landscapes, *Mist in Kanab Canyon* was painted in his New York studio. In 1873 Moran had traveled west with the writer J. E. Colburn, who was gathering information for an upcoming piece entitled "Cañons of the Colorado" for the sumptuously illustrated publication *Picturesque America.*

Using sketches he had made and possibly photographs John K. Hillers had taken during the trip, Moran began this painting in 1880. He continued working on it in 1881 and finished it in 1882. Despite the painting's apparent fidelity to nature, Moran insisted, "my general scope is not realistic; all my tendencies are toward idealization."

Mist in Kanab Canyon is a magnificent example of Moran's idealized representation of the breathtaking rock formations and atmospheric effects he had witnessed. This epic landscape—composed of shifting diagonals and verticals rendered in subtle shades of purple, brown, and green—possesses a primordial quality. The lone limestone pinnacle stands, in swirling patches of sunlight and fog, as if to guard against further encroachment.

Aurora Borealis, by
Frederick Edwin Church,
1865, oil on canvas.
NMAA

Frederick Edwin Church (1826–1900) was a landscape artist and naturalist, as well as a great traveler. In 1859 he visited Labrador and Newfoundland in the Arctic. As was his practice, he made many oil sketches for the subsequent production of more substantial works in his studio. Church incorporated the sketches and observations from this trip into several paintings, including *Aurora Borealis* in 1864.

A striking natural phenomenon that took place during the final phase of the Civil War inspired Church to resurrect his Arctic sketches. On December 10, 1864, General Sherman had reached the sea after ravaging Georgia, and General Thomas had decimated Hood's army in Tennessee on the 15th. On December 23, millions of northerners witnessed the majestic display of the aurora borealis. Many saw the spectacle as a sign of their approaching victory. Church's masterpiece is a testament to the symbolic power of that event.

Corn, A Miniconjou Warrior, by George Catlin, 1832, oil on canvas. NMAA

George Catlin (1796–1872), a lawyer and portraitist, became fascinated with Native American cultures when he saw a delegation arrive in Philadelphia in the 1820s. He was so impressed with the group's dignity that he decided to assist in the preservation of Native American culture and history. Painting Native Americans' portraits, recording their traditions, customs and ceremonies, and collecting examples of their artifacts became his life's vocation. Catlin believed, as did many others during the 19th century, that Native American cultures would soon become extinct. He conceived of his art as a memorial to them.

He painted this portrait of Corn, a Miniconjou Sioux warrior, at Fort Pierre, a military outpost on the Missouri River northwest of Fort Leavenworth, Kansas. There, Catlin painted the portraits of many Sioux people. His depiction of this man is a sympathetic portrait of a great warrior at rest, and he emphasizes the strong planar structure and proud features of his subject's face. Catlin worked in the classical and European tradition of heroic painting and sculpture, using its conventions to pay tribute to his chosen subject.

Thomas Eakins (1844–1916) studied in Paris with Jean-Léon Gérôme, one of the foremost mid-19th-century French academic painters. Eakins rejected the idealization and showy historical scenes that characterized his teacher's work. Instead, he developed a more sober, scientifically observant style, especially in his portraits, for which he is most famous. Nonetheless, Eakins never forgot Gérôme's ability to paint his subjects as "living, thinking, acting men, whose faces tell their lifelong story," and strove to achieve the same effect in his own work.

This aesthetic goal is evident in his unflinchingly direct portrait of his wife, artist Susan McDowell Eakins (1851–1938). Painted during a turbulent period when he was accused of personal misconduct, the portrait presents his staunchest supporter gazing wearily out at the viewer. While somber and completely unsentimental, it captures Mrs. Eakins's still reserve and inner strength.

Mary Cassatt (1844–1926), one of the most famous late-19th-century expatriate artists, took up the theme of the mother and child in 1880. After the turn of the century, it became virtually her only subject. She patterned her compositions after Italian Renaissance paintings of the Madonna and Child, figures often accompanied by an infant John the Baptist.

The Caress is a superb variation on this theme. It recalls the compositional formats found in Renaissance sacred art. But its emotional blandness distinguishes it from Old Master depictions of the Madonna and Child. Although the three figures in this painting could not be physically closer, their attitude seems detached. Cassatt underscores this sense of emotional distance by having the figures gaze away from each other. Formal design—not the rendering of emotion—was Cassatt's primary goal, not only in this painting but in others devoted to the theme.

Reacting to the lack of emotion, Edgar Degas said of a similar Cassatt painting, "It is the baby Jesus and his English nanny."

The Caress, by Mary Cassatt, 1902, oil on canvas. NMAA

Mrs. Kate Moore, by John
Singer Sargent, 1884, oil
on canvas. HMSG

A highly prolific artist, John Singer Sargent (1856–1925) is best remembered for his portraiture—especially of wealthy, socially prominent women. Sargent combined highly stylized presentations with unconventional poses, awkward gestures, intent gazes, and a bravura handling of paint in order to convey the personalities of his subjects.

Responding to one critic who found his unconventional approach disturbing, Sargent remarked, "I have very often been reproached with giving a hard expression to ladies portraits, especially when I have retained some look of intelligence in a face." In so doing, he reinvigorated the tradition of the painted likeness.

Mrs. Kate A. Moore, born Katharine Robinson, was a millionairess from Pittsburgh residing in Paris, where she entertained lavishly and defied the condescension of society wits. In the portrait, Sargent depicts an obviously beautiful and wealthy woman in a strangely twisted pose, ingeniously representing not only her personality but also her somewhat awkward yet commanding status in Parisian society.

Garden in May, by Maria Oakey Dewing, 1895, oil on canvas. NMAA

Born in New York, Maria Oakey (1845–1927) became an accomplished artist and a prolific writer. When she was thirty-six, she married the painter Thomas Wilmer Dewing, known for his portraits and paintings of domestic interiors. So that her work would not compete with her husband's, Maria abandoned her own portraiture to create floral masterpieces, which she cultivated both on canvas and in her extensive gardens.

As a pupil of John LaFarge (1835–1910), famous for his still-life renderings, Dewing shared his enthusiasm for the asymmetrical arrangements, diagonal compositions, and abrupt croppings characteristic of Oriental art. In *Garden in May,* Dewing exhibits several of these stylistic traits, but she adds her own point of view—that of the gardener bending down to the level of the fragrant blooms and sweet earth. Attesting to the value that her practical experience held for her art, Dewing once remarked, "If one would realize the powerful appeal that flowers make to art, let them bind themselves to a long apprenticeship in a garden."

Ferry Slip, Winter, by John Sloan, 1905–6, oil on canvas. HMSG

A native of Philadelphia, John Sloan (1871–1951) studied at the Pennsylvania Academy of Fine Arts and first became known as an illustrator. After he moved to New York in 1904, he began painting urban scenes full time. In a period when patrons, artists, and connoisseurs still turned to Europe for training and largely accepted European aesthetic conventions, Sloan and several other artists developed a new brand of American realism based on their observations of everyday city life. Originally known as "the Eight," Sloan's group was later dubbed, somewhat disparagingly, the "Ash Can School" because of the gritty realism of these artists' urban scenes and their preference for dark colors.

Sloan painted *Ferry Slip, Winter* when he was still new to, and awed by, New York City. He described the ferry as "an antique friend of the commuter fighting its way to berth against the mass of packed ice on a blustery winter afternoon." In this painting, as in others of the period, Sloan sacrificed detail to give a sense of immediacy to the scene. He tended to paint quickly from memory, after walking the streets of New York and "soak[ing] in something to paint," as he described his creative method.

11 A.M., by Edward Hopper, 1926, oil on canvas. HMSG

Edward Hopper (1882–1967) has attained international recognition as one the greatest realist painters in 20th-century America. He originally pursued a dual career in commercial illustration and fine arts after studying in New York and Paris. In 1924, when he was forty-two, he gave up commercial work to become a full-time artist after a successful solo debut at the Frank Rehn Gallery in New York. For the rest of his life, Hopper divided his time between his Washington Square studio in Manhattan and his summer home in Gloucester, Massachusetts.

After initially experimenting with Impressionism, Hopper honed his style to an austere realism. By capturing the harsh light of day or the artificial light of the city, Hopper transformed images of mundane rural and urban scenes into haunting depictions of the isolation and anonymity of modern life. In *11 A.M.*, he contrasts the intimacy implied in a woman's nude body with the impersonal geometry of the city buildings visible through an open window. But he humanizes the apparent impersonality of the scene by using the light streaming through the window to impart a sense of expectant longing to the woman as she gazes out at her urban world.

Photograph of Edward Hopper, by George Platt Lynes, 1950, silver gelatin black-and-white glossy print. AAA

George Platt Lynes (1907–55) began his studies in photographic portraiture during the 1920s and opened a studio in New York in 1933. His photography is marked by an intense concern with formal composition and dramatic light effects. Lynes would manipulate these elements in order to express the essence of his subjects' personalities as he envisioned them.

Lynes took this photograph of the painter Edward Hopper on February 21, 1950, at the artist's studio in New York. He chose to highlight dramatically the artist's hands. The hearth and woodstove behind Hopper balance the shape of Hopper's shoulders.

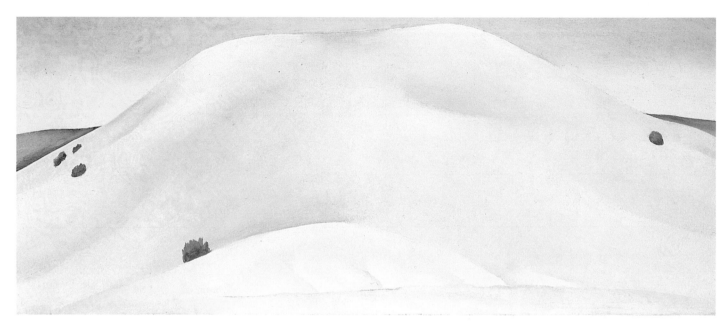

Soft Gray, Alcalde Hill, by Georgia O'Keeffe, 1929–30, oil on canvas. HMSG

Born in Sun Prairie, Wisconsin, Georgia O'Keeffe (1887–1986) began her art training in the traditional academic realistic style and became a commercial artist and art teacher. But her encounters with modern art in 1908 at Alfred Stieglitz's New York gallery led her to a develop a style characterized by bold, simplified forms and strong, pure colors. In 1915 O'Keeffe produced such original abstract drawings that Stieglitz began exhibiting her work in his gallery, presenting her first solo exhibition in 1917. She gave up her teaching career in 1918 to join Stieglitz in New York. They were married in 1924. Over the next fifty years, O'Keeffe divided her time between New York City, Lake George, New York, and New Mexico, where the desert inspired much of her later work.

Natural light, particularly the strong light of the American West, fascinated O'Keeffe. She sought to reproduce its effects on the stripped-down, partially abstract forms she painted. During her first summer at the Taos art colony in 1929, she was overwhelmed by the effects of the bright New Mexican light and the desert's mysterious landscape. In *Soft Gray, Alcalde Hill*—unusual for its muted but still luminous colors—O'Keeffe captures the blue and gray tones of the sun-bleached New Mexican hills and highlights their simple shapes with glowing light.

Photograph of Georgia
O'Keeffe, by Alfred
Stieglitz, 1920, silver
gelatin black-and-white
matte print. AAA

Throughout his career, Alfred Stieglitz (1864–1946) strove to elevate the artistic status of photography in the public's mind. He was a member of the avant-garde in Paris and published some of Gertrude Stein's writings. In 1903 he opened the "291" photography gallery in New York City with his friend and fellow photographer Edward Steichen. There they exhibited not only photographs but also paintings and sculptures by Rodin, Cézanne, Matisse, Picasso, and Brancusi, among others. By displaying these works together, he implicitly asserted that photography had the same artistic status as the paintings and sculptures.

O'Keeffe, with her powerfully honed, expressive, and compelling features—somewhat reminiscent of her painting style—was one of Stieglitz's favorite and most famous photographic subjects. In his words, Stieglitz sought to capture "related shapes and deepest human feeling" in his art. That quality is readily apparent in this haunting portrait.

A member of the famed African American 369th Infantry in World War I, Horace Pippin (1888–1946) became an artist despite a wound that partially paralyzed his right arm. Self-taught, he drew subject matter not only from events in his own life, but also from history and the Bible.

Painted in direct response to World War II, *Holy Mountain III* is the third of a series of four works based on Isaiah 11:6–9: "The wolf also shall dwell with the lamb, and the leopard shall lie down with the kid; and the calf and the young lion and the fatling together; and a little child shall lead them. And the cow and the bear shall feed; their young ones shall lie down together: and the lion shall eat straw like the fox.... They shall not hurt nor destroy in all my holy mountain: for the earth shall be full of the knowledge of the Lord, as the waters cover the sea."

Pippin chose a black shepherd to serve as the redemptive Christ figure that Isaiah had prophesied. Though his peaceable kingdom contains reminders of war and destruction—particularly the series of graves stretching off into the shadows of the wood—Pippin was a deeply religious and hopeful man convinced of the truth of the prophecy of ultimate peace.

Holy Mountain III, by Horace Pippin, 1945, oil on canvas. HMSG

As Auguste Rodin (1840–1917) achieved international fame in the late 19th century, he forcefully asserted his belief that sculpted fragments of the human body could be as expressive as whole figures. He found such expressiveness in the broken sculptures left from Greek and Roman antiquity. The major Romantic sculptor of the period, Rodin transformed the classical tradition of Greece and Rome, as well as that of the Renaissance, to achieve greater freedom of expression.

In 1900 Rodin resurrected the plaster studies for the torso and legs of a work begun thirty years earlier and reassembled them into a new sculpture that became *Walking Man*. He made no effort to hide the force he used to attach the torso to the hips and to remove the head and arms. Those areas openly bear the marks of the artist's hands and tools, stressing the fragmentary quality of the work. The missing anatomical parts and the surface gouges suggest that the figure has survived physical torment and still strides forward purposefully. The work powerfully symbolizes humanity's stubborn perseverance in the face of adversity.

Walking Man, by Auguste Rodin, 1900, bronze. HMSG

Artists Working around the World

Since its founding, the Smithsonian has collected works from a wide range of cultural traditions. Its holdings include, among others, Chinese jades, Japanese porcelains, Indian metalwork, royal Benin bronze plaques, Islamic illuminated manuscripts, and Native American ceramics. The objects shown here provide a lens through which we can begin to understand and appreciate some of the ritual ceremonies, daily activities, and aesthetic traditions of people throughout the world.

Bronze and jade objects had enormous prestige in ancient China. Many have survived because people placed them in grave sites or buried them as offerings to spirits. Bronze vessels were used in ceremonies designed to ensure harmony between living people and the spirits of their deceased ancestors. Ancient bronze vessel forms are based on traditional pottery forms.

Prominent in this vessel is the decoration featuring the *taotie*—a ferocious mask with large eyes and shapes suggesting horns, fangs, and ears. The precise meaning of this motif, which became popular during the Shang dynasty between the 15th and 10th centuries B.C., is unknown. An abstract depiction of a human figure appears above one of the *taotie.*

Ritual food vessel (*li-ding*), China, 12th–11th centuries B.C., Shang dynasty, bronze. AMSG

Finial with birds, Sinú cultural group, Colombia, 1000–1600 A.D., gold. NMAI

This finial, or staff head, is one of the largest lost-wax castings from the Sinú archaeological zone. The Sinú peoples lived close to the Sinú River in the lowlands of what is now northwestern Colombia. When the Spanish arrived in the region in the 16th century, they found the area rich in gold.

Sinú artists perfected a realistic style of gold sculpture in order to communicate their perception of the natural world around them. This finial is a superb example of those artists' skill. The staff head was designed to slip onto a wooden rod that has disappeared, probably because of the effect of the damp climate of the Colombian lowlands on organic materials. The rod would have been too thin to support any heavy weight. For this reason, and because the birds are best viewed when the object is held horizontally, the finial probably served as the finger grip of a wooden spear thrower with a ceremonial rather than a practical function.

This box has an eight-sided body and lid constructed of silver openwork. Its maker decorated it with scrolled floral designs interspersed with birds, chased and engraved details, and gilded borders. The handle terminates in two dragon-heads *(makara)* facing each other. The pierced openwork and floral decoration are hallmarks of Deccani metalware, which was produced in the central plateau region of southern India.

Boxes *(pan-dan)* like this contained *pan,* an Indian delicacy composed of crushed betel nuts, spices, and lime rolled together and enclosed in the leaf of the betel plant. The custom of offering and eating *pan* was an important social ritual widespread throughout India for centuries. The artisan designed this richly decorated container to indicate the high social status of its owner to guests partaking of the *pan.*

Box for betel nut and spices *(Pan-dan)*, India, 18th century A.D., gold and silver. AMSG

The clearly defined muscles, exaggerated horns, and strongly modeled face of this ibex are typical of Iranian sculpture from the second millennium B.C.. The ibex is one of the most frequently portrayed animals in ancient Near Eastern art. It appears on ceramic vessels, cylinder seals, and stamps.

The purpose of this figure is unknown, although it, along with a matching figure, might have been used as a decorative fitting on a piece of furniture, perhaps a throne. The figure has holes for attachment on its head, chest, and feet, as well as incised markings on only one side of its body. This may indicate that one side was more prominent or visually accessible than the other when placed in its intended setting. Figures of animals such as gazelles made of metal or other valuable materials often decorated furniture in ancient Egypt and the Near East.

Goat or ibex, Iran, Bronze Age, 1000–800 B.C., bronze and stone. AMSG

Water dropper, China, 17th–19th centuries A.D., Qing dynasty, jade (nephrite). AMSG

Jade usually refers to either nephrite or jadeite, both hard stones difficult to shape. Ancient sculptors did not so much carve jade as shape it into figures by using abrasives and simple grinding tools. Given the arduous, time-consuming labor involved, the delicate forms, intricate designs, and high polish of ancient pieces are all the more remarkable and indicate the high esteem that the Chinese had for the material's beauty.

An animal with a split tail emerging on the opposite side of the vessel supports this vase consisting of two cylinders. A bird with outspread wings stands atop the animal's head. The artist embellished the surfaces of the two cylinders with deliberately archaistic spiral and plant motifs that had first appeared in China during the Zhou dynasty between 1051 and 221 B.C. The artist's decision to use traditional motifs developed more than 1,000 years earlier testifies to his reverence for tradition—a cultural trait evident in practically all Chinese art.

In spite of its fierce appearance, intensified by its large teeth and curling horns, this fantastic creature holds a fragile cup in its mouth with a delicacy that suggests a remarkably benign temperament. The circular opening on the animal's back allowed the owner of the jade to fill the interior chamber with water. Small amounts of water then trickled through the small opening in the animal's mouth into the oval cup.

A jade of this size and complexity would have been an especially prized object on the desk of a Chinese scholar, where it would have provided the water he could mix with ground ink in order to write calligraphy. The reliance on archaic forms in the figure—the shape of the striding animal and the oval "winged" cup have parallels in jades of preceding dynasties—reflects the antiquarian interests of the maker and the jade's owner.

Double vase *(yingxiong ping)*, China, 14th–16th centuries A.D., Ming dynasty, jade . AMSG

The high quality of the material and its refined workmanship make this disk an outstanding representative of Qing culture and taste. The elaborate openwork outer ring surrounding the small disk in the center consists of two dragons. They rise to confront the two large characters at the top that read *chang le* ("long-lasting happiness"). This auspicious sentiment was also the name of a palace building constructed during the Han dynasty (206 B.C.–A.D. 220).

The jade worker's choice of these characters is typical of 18th-century Chinese culture, which is known for its intense fascination with ancient history. Disks themselves— known as *bi*—are a traditional form with an ancient history. Disks crafted for ritual purposes appeared in China as early as the late Neolithic period, between 5000 and 1700 B.C.

Ornamental disk, China, 18th century, Qing dynasty, white jade (nephrite). AMSG

Slit gong, Lobala, Yangere, or neighboring peoples, Zaire or the Central African Republic, 20th century, wood. NMAfA

BELOW: Ownership of elaborately carved slit gongs was widespread among chiefs in northern Zaire and the southern part of the Central African Republic. This monumental slit gong carved in the form of a stylized animal, probably a buffalo, was crafted from a single piece of wood.

Craftsmen form slit gongs by hollowing out a log through a long, narrow opening. The walls of the hollow chamber vary in thickness. The thick side emits lower tones when struck, and the thin side produces higher tones. Slit gongs are played with sticks that sometimes have padded ends. Because slit gongs produce a wide range of tones, they can mimic the sounds of speech. People use them both to transmit messages over long distances and to play music.

Rachel Namingha Nampeyo (1902–85) created and painted this bowl. She was a granddaughter of Nampeyo, the Hopi-Tewa potter from Hano on First Mesa in Arizona who revived the traditional art of pottery making in the early 20th century. Nampeyo taught her skills to her own daughters, who passed the knowledge on to Rachel Nampeyo. These three generations of Hopi women have used their artistic skills and aesthetic imaginations to give new life to an ancient, nearly lost craft.

In her own works, Rachel Nampeyo preserved traditional forms and designs and re-created many of her grandmother's patterns. But her mastery of form and the beauty of her painted lines are indelibly stamped with her own artistic vision.

Hopi vessel, by Rachel Namingha Nampeyo, Arizona, 1950–60, polychrome ceramic. NMAI

Manuscript page from the *Kitab fi ma'rifat al-hiyal al-handasiyya*, by Al-Jazari, Egypt, A.D. 1354, Mamluk dynasty, watercolor, ink, and gold on paper. AMSG

The *Kitab fi ma'rifat al-hiyal al-handasiyya (Book of Knowledge of Ingenious Mechanical Devices)*, popularly called the *Automata,* is devoted to the explanation and construction of 50 mechanical devices, or automatons. Each section of the book describes the components necessary for their construction and their functions. The artist who created the illustrations for the book invested the figures with a sense of movement and life suggestive of the dynamic nature of the devices.

On this page al-Jazari (active late 12th–early 13th centuries) is discussing the construction of vessels and figures used during drinking sessions. People used the automaton depicted here for entertainment at formal gatherings. After removing the figure's cap, servants could pour wine into a reservoir inside its head and then bring the automaton before guests. After several minutes the liquid, flowing through a series of concealed tubes, would begin to fill the goblet held in the figure's left hand, to the delighted surprise of the onlookers. The detailed drawings at the bottom of the page describe the construction of the various components of the device.

Henri Vever was a celebrated jeweler in turn-of-the-century Paris. Through the Maison Vever, he designed and exhibited his own jewelry and helped shape the *art nouveau* movement. Responding to the expressive intimacy and technical brilliance of Persian and Indian manuscripts and paintings that were then becoming more widely available in Europe, Vever became one of the foremost European collectors of Islamic art. He assembled nearly 500 Persian, Arabic, Turkish, and Indian works. These included full and partial manuscripts and albums, paintings, drawings, calligraphy, and bookbindings. The material now forms the Vever Collection in the Arthur M. Sackler Gallery.

This painting is from an album that Charles Vignier exhibited in Europe at the beginning of the 20th century. It has been popularly known as the *Vignier Album* since at least 1912. The folios are distinguished by their elaborate margins, which depict scenes of hunting and feasting. This page shows the pursuit of courtly pleasures at the top, where a young man offers wine to a woman dancing to the beat of a tambourine. In contrast, at the bottom of the page, a skirmish between warriors is underway. At right center—as if hidden by the panels of arabesque decoration from the other narratives—two lovers huddle, clasping each other.

A Pair of Lovers, manuscript page from the *Vignier Album,* Iran, probably 1590–1610, opaque watercolor, ink, and gold on paper. AMSG

This page is from a illustrated copy of the *Falnama (Book of Divination)*, also from the Vever Collection. The text of the *Falnama* is ascribed to the 6th Shia Imam, Jafar al-Sadiq (702–757). It is a compendium of omens and auguries. Although the manuscript is neither dated nor localized, it is believed to be the product of royal workshops at the Safavid court of Tabriz during the middle of the 16th century. Generally considered the largest Persian manuscript illustrations in existence, their subject matter and accompanying text have been the subject of multiple interpretations.

OPPOSITE: *A Demon Descends upon a Horseman,* manuscript page from the *Falnama (Book of Divination),* Iran (Tabriz), about 1550, opaque watercolor, ink, and gold on paper. AMSG

Set in a lush garden, this idealized scene depicts an elderly woman before two sages. The flat colors, conventional figures, and straightforward composition of this work, also collected by Henri Vever, are typical of paintings associated with the 16th-century Uzbek court at Bukhara, Iran. Court artists there emulated many of the themes and compositions of paintings created in the late 15th century at Herat under the Timurid dynasty. Uzbek rulers had appropriated Timurid works and artists to provide cultural and artistic legitimacy to their rule.

During the the 16th century, however, Bukharan artists eventually created their own distinctive style. On the reverse of this painting is a panel of calligraphy inscribed with the words, "Ali is the sea of eternity. Ali is the successor of Muhammad," referring to the Prophet Muhammad's son-in-law and nephew.

An Old Woman and Two Sages in a Garden, manuscript page, Iran (Bukhara), 16th century, opaque watercolor, ink, and gold on paper. AMSG

Plaque with multiple figures, Edo peoples, Benin Kingdom, Nigeria, mid-16–17th centuries, copper alloy. NMAfA

Staff *(oshe shango),* Yoruba peoples, Nigeria, 20th century, wood, glass beads, and pigment. NMAfA

Yoruba worshippers use this type of staff in ceremonies honoring Shango, a deified king whose judgments against evildoers are associated with the destructive power of thunder and lightning. The unknown sculptor of this staff has carved the figure in a relatively naturalistic style. The highly emphasized breasts and the baby on the woman's back symbolize fertility. The kneeling woman represents a devotee of Shango. She gives thanks for her child, a blessing from the god.

The once-powerful kingdom of Benin flourished from 1300 to 1897, when the king was deposed and colonial rule began. At the Benin court, brass casters made plaques exclusively for powerful and wealthy sacred kings. Approximately 900 plaques have survived. Scholars believe that they embellished the piers that supported the roof of the royal palace. The plaques were cast in copper alloy—a material associated with Benin kings, who controlled foreign trade.

This plaque depicts a king *(oba)* flanked by musicians and an attendant raising a ceremonial sword in salute. The relative size of the figures symbolizes their social status—the larger the figure, the higher the rank of the person it represents in Benin society. The half-figures in the upper corners depict Portuguese traders. The Portuguese began trading with the Edo peoples in the late 15th century.

Cylindrical vessel with cover, China, 100 B.C.–A.D. 100, Han dynasty, gilded bronze. AMSG

This gilded bronze vessel was probably used for warming wine. Decorative elements on this vessel include the cast animal-shaped attachments, the three bar feet, and the ring handles combined with masks. Free-standing birds perch on the edge of the lid, and a fantastic feline creature forms the loop of the ring on top.

This bell would have been part of a larger set (chime) of bells, each varying in size. Chinese bells were hung by their suspension loops on frames that were usually made of wood. A single bronze bell, like this one, produces different tones depending on where one strikes it. A full chime was capable of producing an extraordinary range of tones. Chinese bronze workers decorated bells with a wide range of designs, from animals crafted to form the loop of a bell to panels of intertwined dragon motifs placed along a bell's bottom edge.

Musicians played ritual music on chimes at ancient Chinese courts on ceremonial and state occasions. In 1994 archaeologists discovered a large set of sixty-four bells in the 5th-century-B.C. tomb of the Marquis Yi of Zeng in central China. This bell still produces sounds close to, if not identical with, those heard by the original audience. It reveals to us both the elaborate beauty of ancient Chinese music and the fine, exacting craftsmanship of the bell makers.

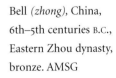

Bell *(zhong)*, China, 6th–5th centuries B.C., Eastern Zhou dynasty, bronze. AMSG

Japanese Porcelains

These works are from a group of thirty porcelain pieces presented to the Arthur M. Sackler Gallery by the Japan Foundation. They are the work of ceramicists belonging to the Japanese artists' association Issuikai, founded in 1936. A tradition of such associations goes back to Japan's Meiji period (1868–1912). The first associations were made up of artists and sculptors. Ceramicists began forming associations in the early 20th century. All Japanese artists' associations mount exhibitions of their members' work.

The works given to the Sackler Gallery represent several locales where porcelain has been made for centuries. The potters use local clays and glazes, and draw upon traditional styles of decoration developed in these areas. These ceramicists place great importance on mastering their chosen techniques of decoration. Ultimately, however, they value expressiveness above cold precision.

"The raw material for the porcelain body of this jar included china stone with enough iron to add a reddish yellow tint. The glaze was mixed from a small percentage of that same china stone, ash of *isu [Distylium racemosum],* wood and iron oxide. It was thickly applied and fired in fairly heavy reduction [limited oxygen]. The iron in the clay and the glaze combined to produce a green glaze with an agreeable texture and soft color. The glaze appears darker where it has pooled in the grooves that I incised in the leather-hard form."
—Sagawa Iwao
(b. 1933)

Jar, by Sagawa Iwao, Japan, 1991, porcelain with green glaze. AMSG

Vase, by Taka Akira, Japan, 1992, porcelain with silver foil and platinum powder under blue glaze. AMSG

"My work includes many pieces based on sketches from nature. I use gold or silver leaf to depict those themes and finish with colors that complement the design. The extremely complex process requires six firings and takes considerable skill. I also pay attention to the effect of the gold and platinum enamels. Finally this process has produced some satisfactory pieces, from which I will now move on to the next level."

—TAKA AKIRA (b. 1936)

Plate, by Hazama Koichi, Japan, 1992, porcelain with enamels over colorless glaze . AMSG

Vase, by Higashi Kuniaki, Japan, 1990, marbleized polychrome porcelain. AMSG

"I shaped this plate from local Kutani porcelain clay and used Kutani-style colored enamels to depict a rural landscape of the Kaga region, where I live. The early autumn scene in a farming village incorporates the yellow of ripening rice, the red and black of the farmhouse roofs, and the blues and greens of trees, distant mountains, and sky. I started with a sketch from nature and aimed for harmony of the enamel colors strengthened by details drawn in black pigment."
—HAZAMA KOICHI (b. 1945)

OPPOSITE: "As an artist of Ishikawa Prefecture, I use a marbleizing technique to extend the possibilities of the Kutani clay and color scheme. I tint the clay different colors, roll the colored clay together, and cut patterned slices from the rolls. I build the basic shape from all the patterned slices. Throwing that shape on a potter's wheel can produce regular designs or spontaneous motifs, depending on the degree of distortion of the patterns in the slices. In this piece I wanted to convey a sense of expansion. I wrapped gradations of blue around my favorite color, pink. I hope the finished pattern suggests blossoming flowers."

—HIGASHI KUNIAKI

(1941–92)

Bowl, by Yoshita Minori, Japan, 1992, porcelain with gold leaf and enamel.
AMSG

"The ornamental technique of applying gold under enamel was developed by Kutani ceramic artists in the 1950s. It involves applying gold leaf or gold pigment to the surface of the high-fired porcelain, covering the design with transparent colored enamel, and firing the vessel once again. I chose a balanced combination of green and yellow enamels, fired first, as the ground for the design. I used thick gold leaf for the clematis flowers and thin gold leaf for the foliage. I coated the complete design with clear glaze and fired once again. The effect of the finished piece depends on the match of the enamel colors and the gold leaf."

—YOSHITA MINORI

(b. 1932)

Transforming the Ordinary

Design is a marriage of form and function that inspires us to look at everday objects from fresh points of view. The geometric lines of a chair, the rich colors of a quilt, and the intricacy of wearable art and jewelry—design elements like these awaken us to the beauty inherent in practical things.

Ewer, Iran, 500–700 A.D., Sasanian period, silver and gilt. AMSG

This ewer, with its hammered and chased details, belongs to a group of vessels derived from late antique forms whose shape was introduced during the late Sasanian period. The foot, handle, lid, and rings on the ewer were cast separately. Dancing women—some clothed, others nude—decorate the sides of the ewer.

Some believe that the dancers (bacchantes) are representations of Anahita (the Zoroastrian goddess of water and fertility) or one of her priestesses or are devotees of a Dionysian cult. It is also possible that these flamboyant women—who hold bowls of fruit, drinking vessels, and other objects associated with prosperity—personify seasonal festivals. Their qualities reflect the assimilation of Dionysiac motifs into the repertoire of Sasanian designs. These elegant and costly vessels were owned by a wealthy elite who used them on festive occasions.

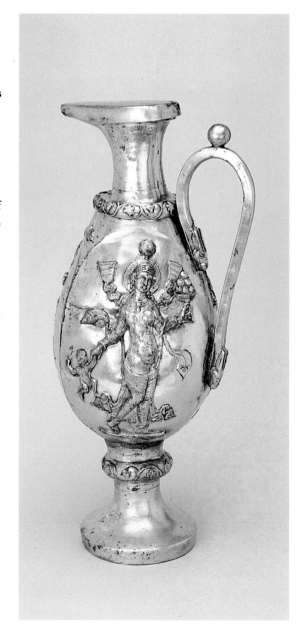

Frederick Miller (b. 1913) forged this graceful pitcher by hand from a silver disk 6 inches in diameter. The pitcher reveals his love of smooth, flowing surfaces and simple, curving shapes. Like many silversmiths of the 1950s, Miller was strongly influenced by modern Scandinavian design.

But Miller pushed beyond the Scandinavian stress on pure symmetry to create bowls and pitchers with slightly irregular shapes inspired by nature. The off-centered design of the pitcher's handle adds a dynamic quality to the work by suggesting the movement of a human hand.

Pitcher, by Frederick A. Miller, 1961, United States, sterling silver with ebony handle. RG

Ralph Bacerra (b. 1938) transformed this teapot—an age-old ceramic format—into a fantastic work of sculpture. The handle appears to be constructed from a series of twigs, and the pot seems to rest on a rough-textured rock. In order to achieve an extraordinarily complex visual result, the craftsman has combined a variety of geometric decorations, both under and over the glaze.

Contrasting colors, textures, and shapes are essential elements in Bacerra's imaginative aesthetic. A sense of humor and playfulness are also apparent in this teapot, for he has designed it so that it appears to be on the verge of tipping over.

Teapot, by Ralph Bacerra, 1989, United States, glazed porcelain. RG

Takoage, by Yvonne Porcella, United States, 1980, machine-pieced and hand-quilted cotton fabric. RG

In the early 1980s, Yvonne Porcella (b. 1936) gave up her career as a practical nurse to pursue her craft full time. A self-taught fiber artist, she began creating art quilts that expressed her fascination with bold, rich colors. Her compositions are largely abstract, made up of long strips, squares, and triangles of vivid cotton fabrics.

Takoage was the first of Porcella's quilts designed to be hung on a wall. In it, and in other quilts, she has produced dazzling, even startling combinations of saturated hues suggestive of strong emotions. Depending upon her imagination, Porcella combines painted, dyed, or printed textiles to evoke quiet moods or to express strong feelings.

Tudor coin-encrusted
tables, by Cheryl Riley,
1993, wood, copper leaf,
coins, brass, and gold leaf.
CH

The American industrialist Andrew Carnegie originally owned this Tiffany table lamp. Lamps with leaded-glass shades were extremely popular between 1900 and the late 1920s. Tiffany Studios made the first and finest of these lamps, which were later widely copied by other, often less-skilled, craftspeople.

A series of dragonflies and gemlike encrustations composed of colored glass embedded in a network of metal dominates the shade of this lamp. The dragonflies seem to hover over the gilt bronze base of the lamp, modeled to look like a pond with lilypads and a tuft of tall grass. The sensitive treatment of the overall design, as well as the sculptural details and rich hues of the glass, are all characteristic of the work produced by the studios founded by Louis Comfort Tiffany in 1900.

Dragonfly table lamp, by
the Tiffany Studios,
1900–1910, United States,
bronze, glass, and lead.
CH

Have a Seat

The four chairs in this grouping combine a practical purpose with their makers' aesthetic visions and provide us with insight into the lives of the people who made and used them. The Ngombe chair may not appear comfortable, but its maker designed it to symbolize the social status of the person who occupied it. Frank Lloyd Wright's chair combines elements of Japanese aesthetics with his own vision of furniture and architectural design. Frank Gehry's lounge chair amuses and startles us by combining a conventional form with an unconventional material. Mecene Jacques drew on legends from his Caribbean heritage to create this hand-made chair in the form of a mermaid and transformed furniture into sculpture.

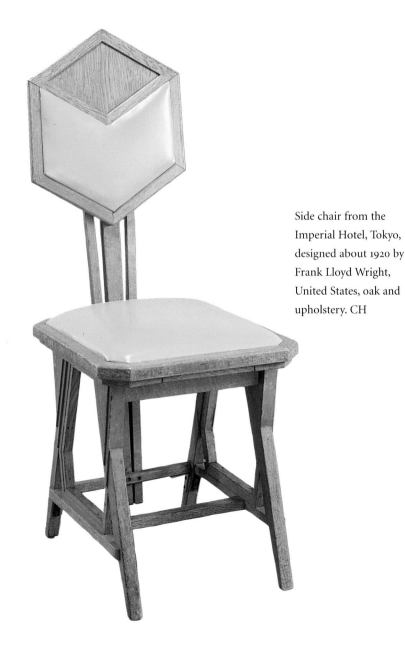

Side chair from the Imperial Hotel, Tokyo, designed about 1920 by Frank Lloyd Wright, United States, oak and upholstery. CH

Frank Lloyd Wright (1869–1959), one America's greatest architects, considered furniture design to be integral to architectural design. Wright once stated that "the most satisfactory apartments are those in which most or all of the furniture is built in as part of the original scheme. The whole must always be considered as an integral unit." Wright embodied his vision in many of the homes he designed, especially his early "Prairie Houses," which featured stained glass, wooden furniture that was often built-in, metal vases, carpet patterns, and lighting fixtures that he had designed as parts of a unified whole.

Wright's furniture, including this chair, was usually made of oak. When he was commissioned to design Tokyo's Imperial Hotel and its furnishings, he designed this chair for use in several public rooms, including the hotel's Peacock banquet room. The chair's strong geometrical shapes—hexagon, triangle, and square—echo the hotel's architectural details. Wright was strongly influenced by Japanese aesthetics. He visited the country several times, beginning in 1905, and collected Japanese woodblock prints. The hotel and its furnishings combine Japanese and Western design conventions.

Lounge chair, 1970, by Frank Gehry, United States, corrugated cardboard. CH

Corrugated cardboard is an unconventional material from which to make a lounge chair, but Frank Gehry's (b. 1930) creative imagination often combines the commonplace with the unexpected. Both an architect and a designer, he frequently creates architectural structures that incorporate unusual materials like corrugated tin, chain-link fencing, and concrete.

Cardboard becomes extremely strong when it is laminated, as it is in this chair. As a result, it makes a comfortable, lightweight, inexpensive, and quite practical alternative to wood or metal. Gehry designed this chair for industrial mass production. It continues the American architectural tradition of developing innovative solutions to the problem of finding inexpensive and practical materials and techniques for furniture design.

Chair, early 20th century, Ngombe peoples, Zaire, wood, brass tacks, and iron tacks. NMAfA

This chair, a sign of high prestige, probably belonged to an important Ngombe chief. An artist carved the body of the chair and its legs from a single block of wood in the customary African fashion. Using European joinery techniques, he then added the rungs. He also added European brass and iron tacks—trade imports that were highly valued and that indicate the owner's wealth and rank.

Mermaid chair, by Mecene
Jacques, United States,
1995, mahogany. AM

Mecene Jacques was born
in Port-au-Prince, Haiti,
in 1925 and immigrated
to the United States,
where he set up a studio
in Maryland. There
Jacques sculpts furniture
and other objects that
draw on various motifs
from his cultural her-
itage. Jacques carved this
chair in the form of a
mermaid, a common
symbolic figure in parts
of the Caribbean.

Pintades (Guinea Fowls),
about 1950, by Pilipili
Mulongoy (b. about 1914),
Zaire, oil on masonite.
NMAfA

Pilipili Mulongoy specializes in portraying delicate, highly decorative landscapes filled with plants and animals. The backgrounds of his paintings are densely patterned, often with small, equal-sized dots. His works have been exhibited extensively in Zaire and Europe, as well as in the United States. He occasionally collaborates with a fellow student, Ilunga.

Pilipili began his artistic career in 1947, when he enrolled in the Atélier d'Art Indigéne at Elizabethville (now Lubumbashi) in south-eastern Zaire. The school was founded by an amateur painter and retired French naval officer, Pierre Romain-Desfossés, who taught his students to create works based entirely on their own experiences. His students—of whom Pilipili is the best known—ultimately developed a distinctive decorative style.

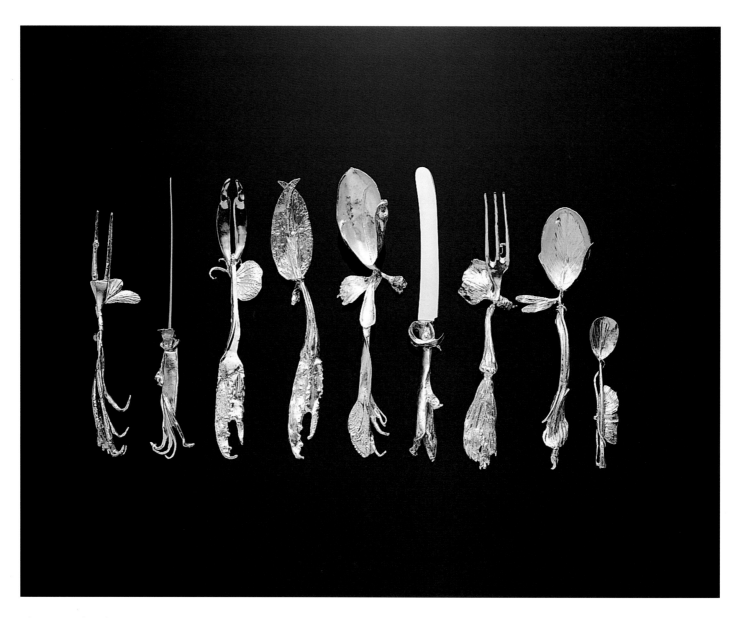

Place setting based on forms of nature, 1966, by Claude Lalanne, France, silver. CH

Claude Lalanne's (b. 1925) work as a sculptor influenced her production of this set of flatware. She based the shape of each piece on natural forms, in some instances taking casts directly from real leaves, twigs, and shells, as well as other natural objects. Her imaginative vision allowed her to transform everyday tableware and ordinary natural materials into art.

Lalanne's work methods closely resemble those of Renaissance silversmiths, who often made castings from leaves, twigs, shells, insects, and small animals like lizards, fish, and frogs. She shares their strongly empirical approach to artistic representation, not only in this silver flatware service but also in her sculpture and the other domestic objects she has crafted.

Place setting from the Imperial Hotel, designed in 1922 by Frank Lloyd Wright, United States, produced in Japan in the 1960s, porcelain with printed enamel decoration. CH

Frank Lloyd Wright conceived of these plates when he was commissioned to design Tokyo's Imperial Hotel and its furnishings. The hotel was completed in 1922 and demolished in 1968. Wright carefully integrated the designs of the hotel's architectural elements with its furnishings, down to even this table service. Such thorough integration was central to Wright's design aesthetic, for he believed that the most beautiful buildings were ones filled with furniture and other objects specifically designed for those settings.

Wright was strongly influenced by Japanese aesthetic traditions, and he married Eastern and Western principles in his designs for the hotel. These plates show Japanese influence in the simplicity and asymmetry of their design, and they demonstrate Wright's interest in abstract forms. The plates appealed to Japanese and Westerners alike, and Noritake produced the design until the 1960s.

Among the Baule peoples, artists cast gold pendants in a variety of forms, including the human face. Important men and women wore the pendants as hair ornaments, suspended them from necklaces, or attached them to caps. Today the Baule cherish these pendants as family heirlooms and wear them on important occasions, such as the installation of a chief, and at receptions for local and foreign dignitaries.

Pendant, Maya peoples, Central America, made between 900 and 1500, jade. NMAI

The Maya—who lived in the jungle regions of southern Mexico, Guatemala, and Honduras—were expert artisans who created exquisitely detailed carvings in jade. They considered jade more valuable than gold, for it possessed a deep symbolic meaning in their culture: its green color represented water and therefore life itself. They often placed small pieces of jade in the mouths of the dead to ensure their spirit's survival.

This head-shaped pendant demonstrates the craftsman's skill in combining naturalistic details with traditional forms of stylization. One gains a powerful sense of the subject's strong personality, manifested especially in the determined cast of his mouth. Thus the artisan successfully combined traditional forms with his own perception of his subject's inner nature.

Merriweather Post tiara and brooches, United States, early to mid-19th century, diamonds and white gold. NMNH

Artisans who make jewelry strive to create settings that enhance the natural beauty of gems. The designer of this mid-19th-century set designed a spring-mounted setting, called a tremblant, that allowed the diamonds to capture and reflect light whenever the wearer moved. Marjorie Merriweather Post, the cereal heiress, owned the set.

Star of Bombay, star sapphire from Sri Lanka. NMNH

The Star of Bombay is one of the world's great star sapphires. The actor Douglas Fairbanks, Sr., gave it to his wife, silent-film actress Mary Pickford. Light reflecting off parallel bundles of tiny needles of the mineral rutile inside the sapphire's crystal structure produces the starlike effect. The artisan who cut and polished this stone into a cabochon—a smooth, rounded shape—had to discern the precisely correct orientation for his design in order to bring out the star.

Mackay emerald necklace, designed by Cartier, Inc., United States, about 1930–31, platinum with emeralds and diamonds. NMNH

The Mackay emerald is the largest set emerald in the Smithsonian collection. It is part of an art deco diamond-and-platinum pendant designed by Cartier. In 1931 Clarence H. Mackay presented the necklace as a wedding gift to his wife, Anna Case, a prima donna with the New York Metropolitan Opera from 1909 to 1920.

Flawless emeralds are exceedingly rare. Like most, the large emerald in the Mackay necklace has several cracks and inclusions of other mineral crystals, including parisite. The presence of parisite reveals that the emerald was mined at Muzo, Colombia, the only site known where the two minerals occur together.

Hooker diamonds,
designed by Cartier, Inc.,
United States, late 1980s,
gold with diamonds.
NMNH

A special cut, called a
starburst, gives these
fancy yellow diamonds
their brilliant sparkle.
Light interacting with
traces of nitrogen in the
diamonds' crystalline
structure makes them
appear yellow. Fancy dia-
monds—those with deep
colors like yellow, pink,
blue, and red—are
exceedingly rare and
highly prized. Only about
1 in 100,000 diamonds is
a fancy color.

Together, the fifty
matched diamonds in
this necklace weigh about
245 carats. The earrings
feature two large yellow
diamonds weighing
about 25.3 carats each.
The ring provides the setting for the largest dia-
mond in the ensemble. It
weighs 61.2 carats.

Necklace #1057, by Earl
Pardon, United States,
1988, sterling silver, 14-
carat gold, ebony, ivory,
enamel, shell, ruby, garnet,
blue topaz, rhodolite,
amethyst, and spinel. RG

Earl Pardon's (1926–91)
necklace demonstrates
his remarkable ability to
combine the eye of a
painter with the skills of
a jeweler. The work is
composed of twenty-one
individual rectangles,
each of which he treats as
a miniscule abstract com-
position. On sterling silver plaques, Pardon has
soldered together flat sections of gold with color-
ful enamel, ivory, ebony,
and bezel-set gems to create a series of intricate
collages with subtly dif-
ferent combinations of
shapes and forms.

Pardon once referred
to his jewelry as
"portable art." An influ-
ential teacher and a
major influence on the
development of studio
jewelry in the United
States, he served as a pro-
fessor of art at Skidmore
College for thirty-eight
years.

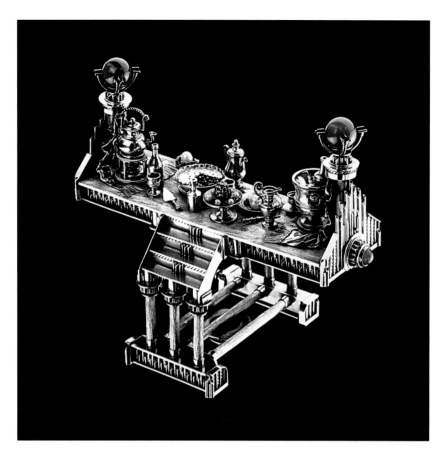

In its intricate detail and exacting craftsmanship, Richard Mawdsley's (b. 1945) sterling silver feast bracelet is similar to masterworks by Renaissance-era goldsmiths. The piece represents a banquet table laden with tiny carved, chased, and turned objects—lamps with jade globes, cloths, knives, forks, goblets, plates of fruit (actually minute pearls), a berry pie, coffee and tea pots, and a bottle of wine in a bucket filled with miniature ice cubes.

Historical motifs intrigued Mawdsley and inspired this piece. He designed the bracelet to be reminiscent of 17th-century Dutch still-life paintings of feast-laden tables that accurately represent details of the table-top setting. The Photo-realist painters active in the 1970s also stimulated Mawdsley's interest in the accurate representation of everyday reality. The bracelet reveals as well the element of fantasy that colors his imaginative vision.

Feast bracelet, by Richard Mawdsley, 1974, United States, sterling silver, jade, and pearls. RG

Amuletic Beads #3, by William Harper, 1976, United States, enamel and pigments. RG

Wilkinson ringdant, designed by A. Z. Palais, early 1960s, United States, gold with diamonds. NMNH

Diamonds bend (or refract) and disperse light in a way that produces an internal fire. This piece possesses a 22-carat emerald-cut center diamond and 5.9 carats of surrounding smaller diamonds composed of 52 tapered baguettes and 24 brilliants. The designer was inspired by the form of a ballerina's tutu. The setting he created is known as a ringdant. The designer fabricated it to be both a ring and a pendant.

OPPOSITE: William Harper (b. 1944) began his career as a painter. But in the early 1960s he changed media, turning to enameling in order to create more intense and fluid colors. He studied medieval and Renaissance cloisonné (partitioned) enamels and reinvented the technique for modern artists. Harper also studied tribal ritual objects from West Africa and pre-Columbian America, and he sought to express their symbolic and magical qualities in his own works. *Amuletic Beads #3* shows Harper's extraordinary range of colors, his technical virtuosity, and his interest in mysterious objects.

Reinventing Tradition

The artists represented in this gallery come from all over the world. Twentieth-century painters and sculptors, like their predecessors in every time and place, use their creative energy to question and transform established conventions.

They develop new styles, exploit new media, and explore nontraditional subject matter. The Smithsonian collects and exhibits the work of contemporary artists, documenting their diverse and continually changing aesthetic goals.

Singing Head, by Elizabeth Catlett, 1980, black Mexican marble. NMAA

Born into a comfortable middle-class neighborhood in Washington, D.C., Elizabeth Catlett (b. 1919) attended public schools and earned her degree from Howard University in 1936. Technically, she has been influenced by African woodcarving as well as pre-Hispanic and Mexican stone carving and ceramic sculpture. For her the artist's role is defined by the nature of human character. She once observed that "artists should work to the end that love, peace, justice, and equal opportunity prevail all over the world; to the end that all people take joy in full participation in the rich material, intellectual, and spiritual resources of this world's lands, peoples, and goods." That moral vision is apparent in her artistic creations.

Since the 1940s, Catlett has chosen to create fairly abstract forms rather than strictly naturalistic representations in her prints and sculptures. Her investigation of the face, which she considers a key to racial identity and a record of human experience, dates from that period. *Singing Head* displays all of these features with its sleek planes, abstract contours, and innate vitality.

Head, by Pablo Picasso,
1934, oil on canvas. HMSG

Pablo Picasso (1881–1973) was one of the most energetic and productive artists of this century. For more than seven decades, he explored his favorite themes in different styles and media, often simultaneously. His genius lay in his invention of new ways to evoke visual experiences of the modern world while also drawing on the history of art for inspiration.

In *Head,* a portrait of his mistress of that period, Marie-Therese Walter, Picasso uses the multiple-view technique of Cubism. He had invented the style with the artist Georges Braque twenty years earlier. At that time, Picasso's friend the poet Guillaume Apollinaire defined it as "the art of depicting new wholes with formal elements borrowed not only from the reality of vision, but from that of conception. . . . in cubism, the geometrical surfaces of an object must be opened out in order to give a complete representation of it." Here Picasso depicts Walter's blond, voluptuous beauty in the curves of her breasts and cheeks, which are fragmented, reshaped, and integrated into the forms of Cubism.

Fernand Léger (1881–1955) became a leader of the Parisian vanguard between the two world wars. Originally trained as an architect, he worked as an apprentice and draftsman for five years before he turned to painting in 1903. His work ranged in style from the multiple perspectives, geometric forms, and shifting color planes of Cubist painting to the more austere geometry characteristic of Purism.

Still Life: King of Diamonds belongs to a series of paintings Léger based on the motif of the playing card. While precisely representing the tarot card figures, he transformed the emblems of an old-fashioned card game into machine parts. In this work, as in many of his figure paintings and still-life scenes, Léger created analogies between the classic ideal of harmony and his own utopian dreams of a rational machine age. By melding classical design elements with representations of modern machinery, Léger became one of the principal architects of 20th-century machine aesthetics.

Still Life: King of Diamonds, by Fernand Léger, 1927, oil on canvas. HMSG

Hot Beat, by Gene Davis,
1964, acrylic on canvas.
NMAA

In the 1960s Gene Davis (1920–85) became a leader of the Washington Color School, a loosely connected group of Washington, D.C., painters who created abstract compositions in acrylic colors on unprimed canvas. *Hot Beat* exemplifies the style of Davis's intensely colored, hard-edged, equal-width stripe paintings. In these works, Davis experimented with complex color schemes that lent themselves to sustained periods of viewing. He suggested that a viewer should "select a specific color . . . and take the time to see how it operates across the painting." Though carefully orchestrated, Davis created his compositions in an improvisational manner. "I paint by eye, " he said, "the way a musician plays by ear."

Photograph of Yasuo
Kuniyoshi, by Max Yavno,
silver gelatin black-and-
white glossy print. AAA

At the age of seventeen, with little money and less knowledge of English, Yasuo Kuniyoshi arrived in Seattle. He supported himself with a variety of odd jobs and soon moved to Los Angeles, where he enrolled in evening art classes. He became a successful artist who realized his desire "to combine the rich traditions of the East with [his] accumulative experiences and viewpoint of the West." He argued that all art was universal, saying that "the stuff from which art is made, feeling, intuition and imagination, is part of all people everywhere."

Max Yavno (1911–85) became a professional photographer in the 1930s. He and his colleagues were united in their commitment to use documentary photography to effect social change. Yavno rarely devoted himself to creating photographic portraits of people. His decision to photograph Kuniyoshi was a fortunate exception in his career.

Born in Japan, Yasuo Kuniyoshi (1893–1953) immigrated to the United States as a teenager. He became an artist schooled primarily in the Western tradition. He incorporated Renaissance, American primitive, and modern influences into his work to attain a brooding style entirely his own. In a rich, dark range of colors that he lightened with blues and pinks during his last decade, Kuniyoshi most frequently depicted the people and scenes of New York and Maine, where he lived and taught.

Look, It Flies is a work from the final years of Kuniyoshi's career, painted a year after the end of World War II. He placed this central image of a woman in a vast, almost undefined landscape. This space, he felt, was filled with the implications of war, which he described in 1947 as "destruction, lifelessness, hovering between life and death, loneliness." The abrupt change of scale from the woman to the tiny ruins at the left, and the odd juxtaposition of images, such as Kuniyoshi's self-conscious inclusion of himself peering into the scene, demonstrate how the artist reformulates reality while observing the world around him from a distance.

Look, It Flies, by Yasuo Kuniyoshi, 1946, oil on canvas. HMSG

Isamu Noguchi (1904–88) sculpted rock, steel, and ceramic—even paper and string—into forms that ranged from massive to delicate. He produced both portraiture and abstract forms, as well as lamps and landscape architecture. Of Japanese-American heritage, Noguchi often used the conjunction of rough and smooth surfaces to express his fusion of Western and Eastern sensibilities in the same object. He was renowned for creating sculptures that could reflect human emotion and thought, as well as allude to nature.

Noguchi created *Endless Coupling* in Japan, at his country house in Kamakura. He had become especially interested in making multiple reproductions, and the technique of iron-casting permitted him to do so. He designed this piece in identical interlocking parts that he could add to whenever he wished. Noguchi was inspired by the structure of railroad couplings when he designed the sculpture, and the title of the work suggests both pulling and pushing, embodying the idea of endlessness. He designed the work as an homage to the Romanian sculptor Constantin Brancusi's earlier abstract sculpture *Endless Column.*

Endless Coupling, by Isamu Noguchi, 1957, cast iron. HMSG

Fernando Botero (b. 1932) paints real-life subjects, but he balloons figures and objects to monstrous proportions in order to draw his audience's attention to the relationships between volume and scale within physical space. His use of exaggerated proportions heightens the witty social satire that characterizes his paintings. Botero takes his subject matter from the small, bourgeois villages of his native Colombia and from Italian Renaissance and Spanish Baroque paintings. He has also been influenced by the Mexican tradition of mural painting. A cosmopolitan artist with deep national ties, Botero has maintained that he is "the most Colombian of Colombian artists."

Despite his use of wild proportions verging on caricature, Botero carefully details the brightly colored and voluptuously rounded forms in *The Hunter*. He depicts his hunter striding through the fall landscape accompanied by a panting little dog. Rabbits dot the hillsides, ignoring and ignored by these predators.

The Hunter, by Fernando Botero, 1980, oil on canvas. HMSG

Richard Estes (b. 1932) frequently bases his paintings on photographs he has taken of urban locations—a technique favored by American Photo-realist painters during the 1970s. But Estes changes aspects of their process by sketching his work onto his canvas rather than transferring photographic images directly onto it. He roughs in his scenes with fast-drying acrylic paint, then switches to oil for the painstaking, highly deliberate work of blending, sharpening, and polishing the image. Estes's changes in basic Photo-realist technique permit him to take liberties with the images he photographs.

Although Estes's paintings appear to be faithful recordings of a site, he sometimes creates entire areas or details within a scene. *Diner* is a study of the strong horizontal and vertical lines apparent in a row of telephone booths he inserted in front of the Empire Diner on 10th Street in Manhattan. Reflections of strong sunlight on glass and metal and the fragmented light and shadows on the sidewalk interrupt the flatness of the image.

Diner, by Richard Estes, 1971, oil on canvas. HMSG

Flowers, by Andy Warhol, 1964, oil and photoserigraph. HMSG

Born Andrew Warhola to Czech immigrant parents, Andy Warhol (1925–87) reached a level of celebrity status that few artists achieve and conceived of his life as his most important work of art. His best-known images were of famous personalities, products, and accident victims, each presented as con- sumable commodities and portrayed with chill- ingly monotonous repeti- tion.

Warhol first used the silkscreen method of transferring a black-and- white photograph to can- vas in 1962. In theory the method is machinelike and removes an artist's brush from the process of creation. However, Warhol's use of large, inexact areas defined by color and of an uneven off-register grid pattern effectively created a painterly image. In *Flowers* Warhol used the same image of a flower within a grid of four silkscreens, each one sub- tly different from the others.

Man and Woman in a Large Room, by Richard Diebenkorn, 1957, oil on canvas. HMSG

Richard Diebenkorn (1922–93) was born in Portland, Oregon, and educated at Stanford University, the California School of Fine Arts, and the University of New Mexico. He taught at both Stanford and the University of California, Berkeley. He completed *Man and Woman in a Large Room* at the height of his involvement with the artists who were part of the Bay Area Figurative Movement. This loosely affiliated group fused the loose brush work of Abstract Expressionism with recognizable subject matter to capture the light and atmosphere of the San Francisco Bay Area.

Through his placement of windows, doorways, glimpses of landscape, and the two figures in a nearly empty room, Diebenkorn demonstrated his interest in strong light effects and the relationship between indoor and outdoor spaces. He structured the painting by a play of parallel and perpendicular lines and by strong foreshortening. The stark simplicity of the room and the anonymity of its occupants recall the work of the American realist painter Edward Hopper.

John Henry, by Frederick
Brown, 1979, oil on canvas. NMAA

In the late 1970s, after a decade of painting abstractions, Frederick Brown (b. 1945) turned to creating portraits of artists and jazz and blues musicians. He also began to paint scenes drawn from urban life and African American folklore.

Brown's *John Henry* celebrates the life of the African American folk hero. Symbolic references to the story of Henry's valiant contest with the steam drill appear in this startling image of the hero directly confronting the viewer while holding his legendary hammer. Although he died from his race against the steam drill, John Henry became a symbol of the struggle many black Americans faced when they moved from an agricultural South to the industrial North.

The Smithsonian's Tucker sedan is the 39th of 51 samples built by the Tucker Corporation in 1948. Preston Tucker (1903–56) intended to mass-produce a "car of the future" with advanced safety, styling, and engineering features. This sedan has its engine in the rear, rubber torsion discs instead of springs, an area where the front passenger could crouch during a collision, and a center headlight that turned with the steering wheel. The aluminum alloy engine is a liquid-cooled version of a Franklin helicopter engine. Producing 166 horsepower, it has six horizontally opposed cylinders. This automobile has an electrically operated manual transmission; a continuously variable automatic transmission also was available.

The avant-garde styling was developed by Alex Tremulis and J. Gordon Lippincott and Company. It is similar to the teardrop-shaped cars of the 1940s, but the center headlight, rear grill, pop-up tail lights, and irregularly shaped windows give the car a futuristic appearance even today. The low profile, tapered fenders, and fast-back shape convey an impression of speed and power and lend the vehicle a distinctly aesthetic quality. The Tucker never went into actual production because a federal investigation into the company's management practices led to the company's collapse.

Tucker automobile,
conceived by Preston
Tucker, 1948. NMAH

Remembering

Only if we remember our past—the important events, the people we love, our country's history, our communities' stories—can we begin to understand the patterns and meanings of our lives. We preserve our memories, like treasures, in our minds. To aid our individual memories, we have created methods of record-keeping, public memorials, and social institutions that preserve our personal and collective past in tangible forms. The Smithsonian itself is an enormous, many-roomed treasure house that performs a function similar to our own memories. The Institution preserves hundreds of thousands of material objects and written records that represent our past and speak to our future.

The objects in the Smithsonian's collections provide us with avenues into other people's lives, beliefs, and thoughts. Their physical qualities bring the past to life. They commemorate momentous events in history as well as the most personal aspects of people's everyday lives. They teach us about the unfamiliar and serve as reminders of our own experiences. They reveal to us the common cultural bonds that unite human beings and reinforce our sense of belonging to a shared community.

Detail of George
Washington's battle sword

Ancient Cultures: Sources of Community

The Smithsonian Institution's collections preserve ancient artifacts from Asia, Africa, Europe, the Americas, and the islands dotting the globe. These artifacts help us learn about the ancient peoples from whom we are descended and serve as testaments to the industry, ingenuity, and creativity of the earliest human communities.

By studying these relics, we can learn about ancient peoples' ways of life—their aesthetic values expressed through art, their use of ritual to strengthen community ties, their development of technologies, their religious beliefs and practices, and their communal activities. These ancient treasures thus reveal the deep historical roots underlying our own communities.

The inhabitants of the Ulúa Valley in Honduras produced exquisitely carved marble vessels prized as luxury items by peoples from northern Guatemala to northwestern Costa Rica. Beginning about A.D. 500, this valley became an important trade route, and these vessels were exchanged throughout the region. Some 150 have survived into our time.

Most Ulúan vessels are cylindrical, like this example, and set on ring-shaped bases pierced with string-sawed designs. This vessel has symmetrical panes filled with finely carved designs including the faces of two deities, serpent heads, and columns of scrolls. A bird figure appears on the bowl's handles. The positions of the bird handles and the deity faces suggest the four cardinal points.

We do not know anything about the possible ritual functions of these vessels. However, the beauty of this piece, and especially the fine symmetry of the overall design that characterizes all known examples of their work, tells us much about the aesthetic vision of the Ulúan peoples.

Carved stone bowl, Ulúan peoples, Honduras, between A.D. 800 and 1200, marble. NMAI

Dagger-ax *(ge)*, China,
13th–12th centuries B.C.,
Shang dynasty, jade.
AMSG

Chinese jade-workers modeled jade dagger-axes after the bronze *ge,* the most commonly used weapon during the Shang and Zhou dynasties—a period of roughly 1,500 years, from 1700 to 221 B.C. Because they are thin and delicate, these jade blades were probably used for ritual functions rather than for battle. Sometimes jade *ge* blades were fitted with elaborately inlaid bronze supports.

The survival of ceremonial implements like this *ge* provide us with some evidence about the elaborate pageantry that characterized ceremonial functions during the Shang dynastic period. We know little about this first Chinese dynasty. Until archaeologists uncovered evidence of the Shang capital city, Anyang, in northern China in 1928, the very existence of the dynasty was doubted.

Clovis points, unidentified peoples, North America, about 9,000 B.C., flint. NMNH

More than 11,000 years old, these Clovis artifacts are among the earliest tools discovered in North America. Clovis projectile points and butchering tools have been found with the remains of ice age animals, notably mammoths, throughout the United States. The tools give us clues about the Clovis people's diets, communal hunting techniques, travel patterns, and possible origins.

Archaeological evidence indicates that the Clovis people attached these weapon tips to lances or spears and probably pursued their prey in hunting parties. These points—with distinctive "flute flakes" removed from both faces around the base—were made of flint gathered from sources hundreds of miles away from the archaeological sites where they were found. Thus the early people who used them must have covered extremely large geographical areas during their seasonal rounds as they followed herds of wild game. Moreover, many of the artifacts are similar to tools found in Siberia, indicating perhaps that the Clovis people descended from hunting and gathering peoples who had migrated from Asia during the last Ice Age.

Cycladic figure, Minoan culture, early Bronze Age, about 2500 B.C., marble. NMNH

The sculptors who made these enigmatic figurines lived on the Cycladic Islands, located in the Aegean Sea between Greece and Turkey. About a century ago, farmers began unearthing them while tilling their fields. Ancient peoples placed the figurines in grave sites, but we know little more about the symbolic meaning that these communities placed on them. The shape of the figures, with their flattened back areas, probably indicates that the sculptors intended for them to lie flat in a grave site. The lack of eyes and mouths, together with the arms folded across the chest, was perhaps intended to suggest the stillness and silence of death. The gender of these figures may indicate that they symbolized either the wives of deceased men or a neolithic mother goddess.

The sizes and styles of these figurines vary enormously. They range from a few inches in height to life-size. Some are among the earliest naturalistic sculptures discovered in the Mediterranean. Others, like this example, are highly stylized and abstract. When they were discovered, the figurines had an immediate impact on European art at the turn of the century, when Abstraction was coming into flower. On viewing one of the Cycladic figures, Picasso is reputed to have said, "No one ever stripped an object that bare!"

Known as the "Swiss Army knife of the Paleolithic Period" (2.5 million to 10,000 B.C.), stone handaxes were the main product of early human technology for nearly one million years. This example was found at the Olorgesailie archaeological site in Kenya, which the Smithsonian investigates in collaboration with the National Museums of Kenya. It dates from the period of *Homo erectus,* the first human species to spread outside of Africa and a close relative of *Homo sapiens.* Similar handaxes have been discovered in Europe, Asia, and Africa. They indicate a uniform pattern of stone technology communicated over a vast area for an immense period of time.

The methods of making handaxes and their uses tell us about the behavior of the earliest humans. Ancient peoples made them by striking large flakes off boulders or by chipping away a rock's circumference. At some archaeological sites, evidence indicates that people used the handaxes to cut meat, animal hides, and plant materials.

Relief panel depicting ballplayer, Maya peoples, Guatemala, A.D. 600–900, limestone. NMAI

Depictions of ballplayers on ceramic decoration and stone wall reliefs were popular among the Maya peoples of Mexico and Guatemala. Large courts devoted to ballgames were common in Maya towns and cities. A peripheral wall decorated with beautiful and complex carved stone panels usually surrounded these courts. This panel was once a decorative element on the façade of such a wall. The ballplayer depicted on this panel wears a chest protector, knee pads, and the headdress of a jaguar god.

The headdress indicates that for the Maya the ballgame was a politically charged ritual as well as a sporting event. They had developed a complex mythology that accorded both rulers and deities complete power over life and death. According to Maya beliefs, the gods demanded constant appeasement. Ball games were an integral part of Mayan sacrificial rituals. The losers of a game, often prisoners captured from a neighboring enemy town for this purpose, were sometimes sacrificed to the gods.

Handaxe, possibly made by *Homo erectus,* Kenya, about 780,000 years old, lava rock. NMNH

Funerary stele, Egypt,
New Kingdom, 18th
dynasty, about 1420 B.C.,
limestone. NMNH

Funerary objects such as this—themselves fashioned as memorials to past lives—attest to the ancient Egyptian community's reverence for the dead, and testify to their sense of the continuity of life through death and beyond. Egyptians placed funerary stelae in tombs in order to ensure an abundance of food, drink, and other necessities for the *ka,* the spirit or soul of a deceased person in the afterlife.

This stele from Matarrya, Egypt, depicts a man and woman, attended by a servant, seated before a pedestal table holding food. Below, another servant looks after jars of beer. The hieroglyphic inscription reads in part: "A boon which the king gives to Atum Lord of Heliopolis and to Osiris, Ruler of Eternity, the Great God, Lord of Abydos, that he may give invocation offerings consisting of bread and beer, oxen and fowl, cool water and clothing, and all good things on which God lives . . . and an old age for the one who placed him in his heart."

Bridge-handle vessel,
Nazca peoples, Peru, A.D.
200–600, polychrome
ceramic. NMAI

Nazca culture developed along the arid coast and valleys of southern Peru between the 2nd and 7th centuries. The Nazca specialized in the production of polychrome ceramic vessels and remarkable textiles.

This vessel has two spouts with a handle between them that resembles a bridge. It probably served an important ceremonial function within the Nazca community, but we do not know what kind. The vessel has a falcon depicted on it—the most important figure in Nazca mythology, perhaps because of its ability to transcend the earth and soar high in the air close to the mountaintops.

Leading the United States

The presidency is the most influential political office in the United States. As the country's highest elected public official, the president protects its citizens' general welfare and guides its international policies. Every president has put his personal mark on the office. The Smithsonian's presidential collections attest to our fascination with the presidency and provide us with tangible links to our leaders. They commemorate the joyous occasions, as well as the challenging times and tragic events our country has experienced in its relatively short history.

The women who have held the powerful, though unofficial, position of first lady have also captured our national attention. Ever since Martha Washington first occupied the position, the women married to American presidents have led lives in which public and private issues are inextricably intertwined.

Some have chosen to play the more traditional role of the nation's hostess, seeing their White House duties as an extension of the supportive social role they played in their marriages. Others have chosen to pursue more activist roles, trying to help solve social problems and promoting the country's good through their unofficial, but very real, political power.

George Washington's battle sword and scabbard, late 18th century, steel, ivory, silver, leather. NMAH

George Washington (1732–99), wore this battle sword throughout his tenure as commander in chief of the Continental Army during the Revolutionary War. J. Bailey (1755–1815), a well-known cutler, made the weapon, basing its design on the English hanger sword. Its steel blade is slightly curved, with a shallow groove running down the center. Silver strips decorate the green ivory grip. The quillons—the perpendicular bar between the grip and the blade—bear a trophy of arms on one side and a similar trophy surmounted by a bear's head on the other.

Samuel T. Washington, one of Washington's nephews, held the rank of captain in the United States Army and inherited the battle sword in 1799. His uncle had charged him to use it only in "self-defense or in the defense of [the] country and its rights."

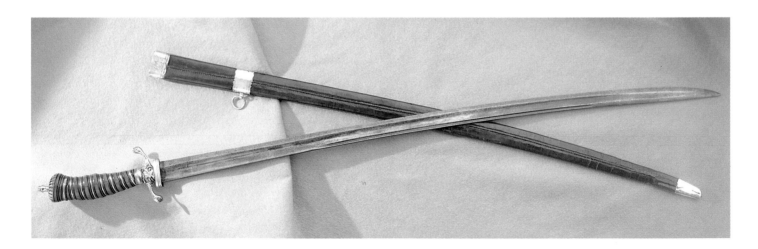

Martha Washington (1731–1802) served the United States as its first first lady and defined the role as one of acting as the hostess of the nation. At her husband's request, she held a "drawing room" every Friday during his presidency between 1789 and 1797. At first referred to as "Lady Washington," Mrs. Washington was somewhat uncomfortable in her role. She described herself as "an old-fashioned Virginia housekeeper." But her self-deprecation was not entirely accurate. She had acted as a mainstay for her husband and his troops throughout the Revolutionary War and invested the position of first lady with great dignity.

Peale based his portrait of Martha Washington on an original painted by his father, Charles Willson Peale, in 1795. That painting now hangs in Independence Hall. To this likeness, Peale added the same stone "porthole" frame that he used for George Washington's portrait. The two were companion pieces, commemorating the Father and the First Lady of the country.

By 1770 George Washington had become a leader in the Virginia House of Burgesses. He served as a delegate to the First and Second Continental Congresses in 1774 and 1775. After he led the Continental Army to victory, Washington presided over the constitutional convention in Philadelphia in 1787. Washington's prestige enhanced the legitimacy of the new government and made his election as the first president almost inevitable.

Rembrandt Peale (1778–1860) painted George Washington from life in 1795. Later in his career, he made many other portraits of the first president based on his memory of the 1795 sitting and on likenesses by other artists. From these, he developed an idealized image of Washington as the *Pater patriae* ("father of the country"). This image served throughout the rest of Peale's life as the model for his famous "porthole" portraits of Washington. In this composition, Washington's idealized face is visble through an oval stonework frame—a convention of European art dating back to the Middle Ages.

Lincoln's political career began in Illinois, and he served four consecutive terms as a state legislator beginning in 1834. He was a member of the U.S. Congress from 1847 to 1849. During the 1850s, Lincoln forcefully spoke out against the expansion of slavery into the western territories. He considered slavery, irrespective of the issue of race, a terrible moral evil. He remained willing, however, to tolerate the continued existence of the institution in the slave states, if that was the price of keeping the country intact.

Lincoln's views made him a moderate in the newly formed Republican Party and led to his nomination as a compromise candidate in the Republican presidential convention in Chicago in May 1860. He was elected on November 6, 1860, with only 39 percent of the popular vote. However, he won a majority of electoral votes—180 altogether—though not a single vote from any southern state.

The Civil War consumed Lincoln's presidency. Despite the defeats initially suffered by the Union army, his resolve to preserve the Union remained firm. Before and during the war, he read military history and helped formulate the Union's eventually successful war strategy. The Emancipation Proclamation that declared the slaves in the seceded states "forever free"—issued on January 1, 1863—was a carefully calculated part of that strategy, and Lincoln justified it as a war measure. He issued it to provide Union troops with a stronger moral motivation to keep fighting, to disrupt further the Confederate economy, and to gain greater support from African Americans, whose participation proved crucial to the final Union victory.

According to tradition, Abraham Lincoln (1809–65) wore this top hat to Ford's Theater on the night of April 14, 1865, when he was shot by John Wilkes Booth. He died the next day.

Abraham Lincoln's top hat, mid-19th century. NMAH

Mary Todd Lincoln's silver service, Gorham Silver Company, about 1859. NMAH

This silver service was probably presented to Mary Todd Lincoln while she was first lady. In a letter dated July 19, 1876, to her son Robert Todd Lincoln, she refers to a silver service in his possession that "the citizens of New York" had given her. The service is Gorham coin silver. The pieces have an overall repoussé floral and strapwork pattern with the monogram "MTL" on one side and an engraved crest—probably an adaptation of the Todd family crest—on the other.

When Mrs. Lincoln became first lady in 1860, the political importance of a skilled White House hostess was well established. A highly educated Kentucky woman, she believed it was her duty to bolster the Union's morale by fostering a brilliant social life in the capital, conducting lavish parties, and refurnishing the White House. But partially because she had the misfortune to come from the South, she became the target of vicious gossip in the wartime capital. People criticized her for "squandering" the taxpayers' dollars and for seeming to show callous disregard for the death and destruction caused by the Civil War.

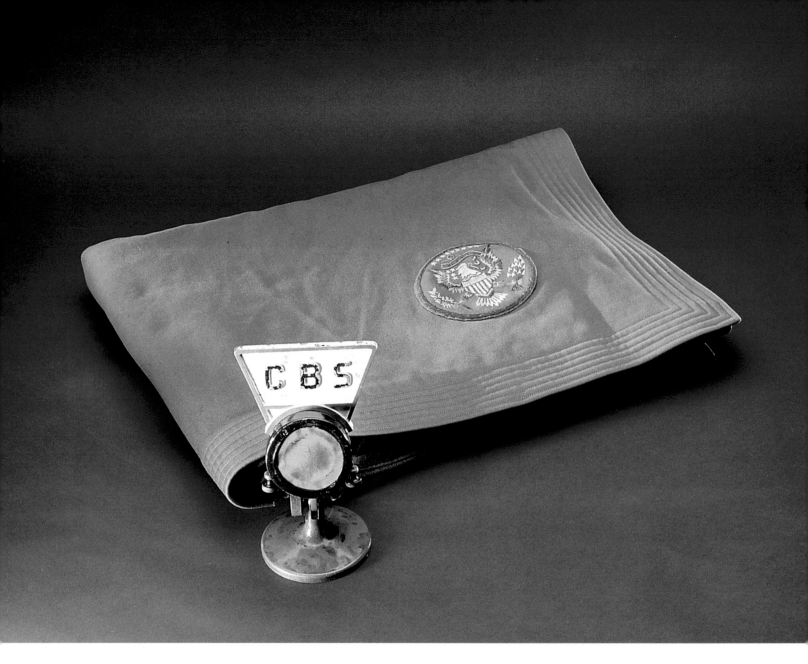

Franklin D. Roosevelt's lap robe and radio microphone. NMAH

Franklin Delano Roosevelt (1882–1945) used this automobile lap robe while he was governor of New York (1928–32), and during his four terms as president (1933–45). It kept his legs warm while he rode in the open cars that he frequently used for public appearances. This was one of the many measures the president took to create a more direct, intimate rapport with the American people as he led the country through the Great Depression and World War II.

Between March 12, 1933, and January 6, 1945, Roosevelt delivered thirty-one of the radio talks he termed "fireside chats." In the first, he addressed the terrifying banking crisis that was taking place during the Depression and explained the implications of the Emergency Banking Relief Act, a measure designed to reopen failed banks. Clyde Hunt, an engineer for some of the addresses, identified this microphone as one of several the president used.

Roosevelt developed an intimate, reassuring rapport with the American people through his talks. Many Americans felt as if he were speaking to them personally. In March 1933, a man from Brooklyn wrote: "What happened last evening as I listened to the President's broadcast, I felt that he walked into my home, sat down and in plain and forceful language explained to me how he was tackling the job I and my fellow citizens gave him."

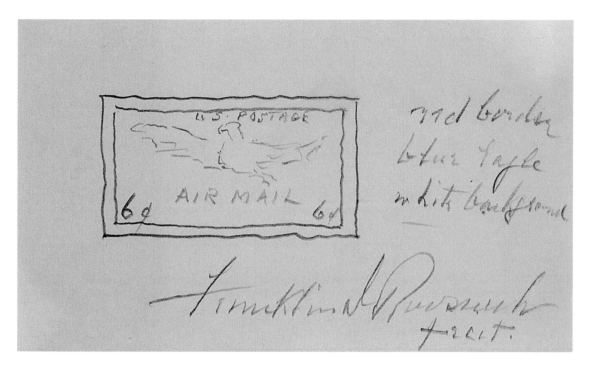

A stamp design sketched by Franklin D. Roosevelt and a 1938 six-cent airmail bicolor stamp based on that design. NPM

Some of the Smithsonian's presidential memorabilia recall our presidents' personal hobbies, evoking the lighter side of history. Franklin D. Roosevelt was a devoted stamp collector and became extremely interested in the post office's issuance of new stamps during his administration.

He sometimes sketched designs for new stamps, including this design for a six-cent airmail stamp issued in 1938. The design of an eagle with outspread wings, holding a shield with arrows and olive branches, symbolizes freedom, protection, and peace. The shield bearing the Stars and Stripes shows the national emblem in conventional form.

No one ever craved the presidency more than Theodore Roosevelt (1858–1919) or used its powers more joyously. In early 1901, however, Roosevelt's steady progress toward that office was suddenly checked. He had risen to national prominence through his "rough-riding" heroics as an officer in the Spanish-American War in 1898, and had been elected New York's governor on a reform ticket in 1900. But fearing his intention to introduce reforms in the state, New York conservatives persuaded him to run as William McKinley's vice president. Roosevelt found himself relegated to a political backwater after McKinley became president in 1901.

McKinley's assasination elevated Roosevelt to the presidency on September 14, 1901. While in office, he was a leader of the Progressive movement, and he worked aggressively to curb the excesses of big business and to conserve the country's natural heritage. Simultaneously, he implemented his policy to "speak softly and carry a big stick" in Central and South America, a policy that climaxed with the building of the Panama Canal.

In 1905 organizers of New York City's Jacob Riis Settlement House commissioned this bronze relief for their gymnasium, where it was meant to serve as an inspiration to the newly arrived European immigrants who used the facility. Sally James Farnham's (1876–1943) sculpture effectively preserves the dynamism of Roosevelt's personality and conveys a sense of it to us even today.

Sculpture of Theodore Roosevelt, by Sally James Farnham, 1906, bronze relief. NPG

Inaugural gown worn by Jacqueline Bouvier Kennedy, 1961, silk chiffon over *peau d'ange*, brilliants, and silver thread. NMAH

First lady from 1961 until her husband's assassination on November 22, 1963, Jacqueline Kennedy (1929–94) projected an image of glamour, youth, privilege, and motherhood. She was well educated in the fine arts, possessed considerable artistic talent, and used White House entertainments to elevate American arts and culture to international prominence. She designed this gown herself, and Ethel Frankau of Bergdorf-Goodman, New York City, executed the design. Mrs. Kennedy wore it to several inaugural balls in January 1961.

After John F. Kennedy's assassination, Mrs. Kennedy orchestrated the country's mourning, helping it recover from the trauma. She personally planned the televised mourning rituals and directed the White House staff to re-create the funeral appointments used when Lincoln was assassinated, thus linking the tragedies. She arranged for a riderless horse to follow the casket in the procession from the White House to the Capitol. Afterward, she played a major role in planning the John F. Kennedy Presidential Library.

Inaugural gown worn by Patricia Ryan Nixon, 1969, designed by Karen Stark for Harvey Berin, New York City, mimosa silk, satin, gold and silver embroidery. NMAH

First lady from 1969 to 1974, Patricia Ryan Nixon (1912–93) supported her husband Richard throughout his political career, beginning with her participation in his 1948 senatorial campaign. In 1952 she cleverly helped Nixon revive his faltering bid for the vice-presidency by appearing on television with their children and their dog, Checkers, to counter political charges regarding questionable campaign gifts.

Mrs. Nixon was a woman possessed of great inner strength, determination, and keen political instincts. Remarking on this aspect of her character, Washington correspondent Helen Thomas once remarked, "She was so much more sophisticated than the Palace Guard I wondered why her husband did not listen to her more often."

Inaugural gown worn by Mamie Doud Eisenhower, 1953, designed by Nettie Rosenstein, Inc., New York City, silk *peau de soie* with pink rhinestones. NMAH

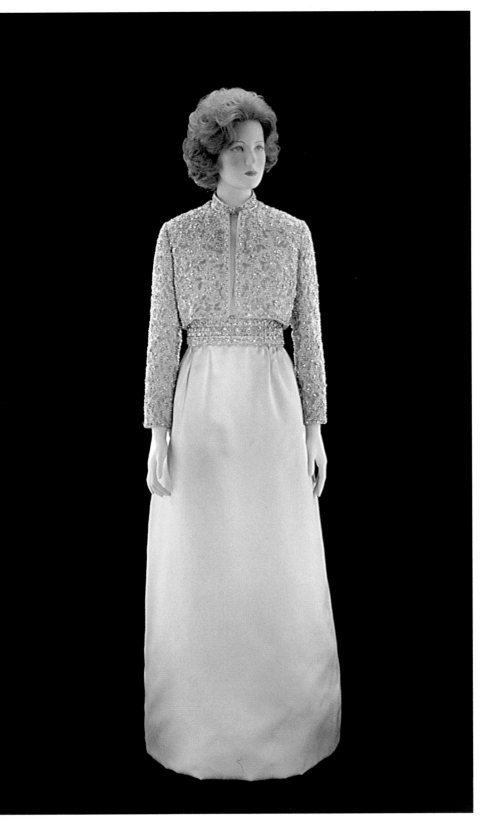

OPPOSITE: During her husband's presidency from 1953 until 1961, Mamie Doud Eisenhower (1896–1979) became one of the most beloved first ladies in history. She had already gained great popularity when she appeared during her husband's first presidential campaign. Chants of "We want Mamie" rivaled those of "We like Ike."

Mrs. Eisenhower defined her primary role as being a successful White House hostess, and her performance was enhanced by her experience as the wife of a high-ranking military officer. Both down-to-earth and dignified, Mrs. Eisenhower personally greeted thousands of tourists visiting the White House during her tenure. The public regarded her as an ideal exemplar of American womanhood in the 1950s, and housewives throughout the country felt that she embodied their own values. Mrs. Eisenhower once described herself as "perfectly satisfied to be known as a housewife."

Inaugural gown worn by Mary Harrison McKee, President Benjamin Harrison's daughter, 1889, made by William Ghormley, New York City, silk brocade. NMAH

Mary McKee (1858–1930) wore this gown to the centennial inaugural ball in the Pension Building in Washington, D.C., 1889. In accordance with President Benjamin Harrison's economic philosophy of "buy American," the gown was intentionally all-American. Indiana artist Mary Williamson designed the fabric pattern, and the Logan Silk Company of Auburn, New York, wove the brocaded fabric. William Ghormley of New York designed and made the gown. A pattern of goldenrod—President Harrison's favorite flower—appeared in the intricately brocaded fabric of the gown.

Inaugural gown worn by
Lucretia Rudolph
Garfield, 1881, oyster satin
and lace. NMAH

Lucretia Garfield (1832–1918) wore this gown to the 1881 inaugural ball. The original color of the gown, described in contemporary accounts, was a delicate lavender. Analysis has revealed that the gown was dyed with fuschine, a light-sensitive synthetic dye that faded to this oyster white.

Like Jacqueline Kennedy, Mrs. Garfield experienced the tragedy of her husband's assassination. James Garfield was shot on July 2, 1881, and lingered painfully for three months while she remained staunchly by his bedside. After his death, she participated in his public memorial services—the first president's widow to do so. Afterward the public donated an unsolicited $360,000 for her and her children's support. She later helped organize and preserve Garfield's political and presidential papers.

Wedding dress worn by
Frances Folsom on her
marriage to President
Grover Cleveland, 1886,
ivory satin, India muslin,
white mull. NMAH

Frances Folsom (1864–1947) married Grover Cleveland in the White House on June 2, 1886. She was only twenty-one and considered very glamorous. Her decision to marry Cleveland enhanced his tarnished image in the eyes of the public. During the vicious 1884 campaign, he had been accused of fathering a child out of wedlock. Cleveland paid child support, but never publicly admitted paternity.

Mrs. Cleveland's popularity with the public led the Democrats to use her attractive image on a vast array of campaign materials during the 1888 election, which Cleveland lost. Her image appeared widely again in the 1892 campaign when Cleveland won the office a second time, making her a potent campaign symbol in her own right.

A House Divided

The Civil War (1860–65) was one of the most critical events—and the bloodiest—in United States history. By 1860 slavery had become one of the great issues that threatened to destroy the Union. All efforts at compromise were overwhelmed by southerners' determination to protect the rights they saw as theirs, growing abolitionist sentiments, and northerners' desire to preserve the Union. Millions of families on both sides suffered direct effects from the drafting and enlistment of nearly 3 million men into the Union and Confederate armed forces. The terrible struggle cost the lives of more than 620,000 men in battle or from wounds and disease. Altogether, more than 1 million people died, were maimed, or lost their health as a result of the war.

This case study of Civil War artifacts demonstrates the manner in which different museums with specific collection aims often focus on the same historic event in different ways. Each of these objects is a treasure in its own right. Together they tell us a more complete story about the Civil War. They allow us not only to recall our collective past but also to draw lessons from those often painful memories.

On February 5, 1865, Abraham Lincoln visited the photographic studio of Alexander Gardner (1821–82), where he posed for a series of portraits, including this one. Gardner used a large glass negative during the process. But despite his skill, the negative broke. Gardner made only a single photograph before destroying the negative.

After Lincoln's assassination on April 14, 1865, the photograph acquired special significance for the public that mourned the loss of its great war leader. The slicing crack in the plate—near the spot on Lincoln's forehead where Booth's bullet struck—seemed to foretell the president's impending assassination.

And though Lee's surrender at Appomattox was still months away when the picture was taken, viewers saw Lincoln's contemplative smile as a weary response to the war's end.

By 1913, when Frederick Hill Meserve acquired this portrait from Gardner's friend Truman H. Bartlett, he believed it to be the very last portrait of Lincoln ever made. Modern historians have proved Meserve wrong, but the myth persists, sustained by the tragic power that Gardner's haunting image still holds for us.

"Cracked plate" photo-
graph of Abraham
Lincoln, by Alexander
Gardner, 1865. NPG

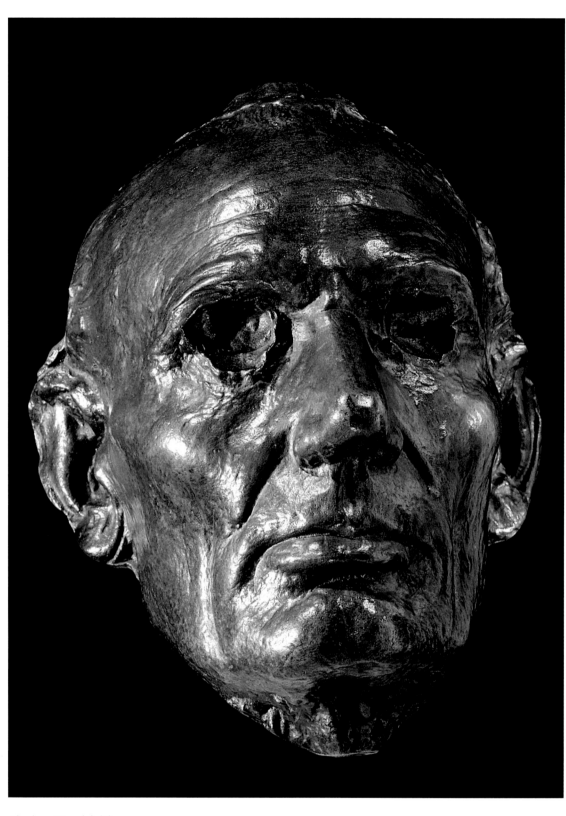

Abraham Lincoln's life
mask, 1886, cast by
Augustus Saint-Gaudens
from an original mask
made in 1860 by Leonard
W. Volk, bronze. NMAH

Leonard W. Volk (1818–95) took a plaster cast of Lincoln's face in Chicago in March 1860, only months before his election. Many southerners interpreted Lincoln's victory as a sign that they had lost power over the federal government. Within a few weeks of his election, seven southern states seceded from the Union. After the attack on Fort Sumter on April 12, 1861, four others joined them to form the Confederate States of America.

Lincoln was committed to preserving the Union and stated that this was his reason for turning to armed force. Over the next four years, he remained unwavering in his determination while he led the war effort. On November 19, 1863, he delivered the Gettysburg Address to commemorate the battle that had taken place on July 1–3. He expressed his firm belief that the country would survive the conflict intact, concluding his speech with these words: "a government of the people, by the people, for the people, shall not perish from this earth."

Photograph of Frederick Douglass, by George K. Warren (1834–84), 1876, albumen silver print. NPG

In August 1841, a young, self-educated runaway slave named Frederick Douglass (1818–95) rose at an antislavery gathering on Nantucket Island to recount his firsthand experiences of the cruelties of slavery. His remarks stirred his audience deeply. By the time he had finished, he had found a new calling. Hired immediately as a paid speaker for the Abolitionist movement, Douglass became one of its most compelling advocates. By the late 1840s, he was well on his way to becoming the most eminent African American of his day.

When the Civil War ended slavery, Douglass's efforts on behalf of African Americans were not over. He soon turned his formidable energy to challenging the many forms of discrimination that continued to deny African Americans their rights. Most often, his pleas for racial justice had little immediate impact. Nevertheless, he left a legacy of determination that became an inspirational underpinning for the civil rights movement of the 20th century.

Appomattox Furniture

On April 9, 1865, the Civil War effectively ended at Appomattox Court House, Virginia, when Generals Robert E. Lee and Ulysses S. Grant met to sign the terms of surrender. On that Palm Sunday morning, when Lee had reached the conclusion that victory was no longer possible, he said, "there is nothing for me left to do but to go and see General Grant, and I would rather die a thousand deaths."

The Union victory ensured that the United States would survive as a single country. Moreover, with the adoption of the 13th Amendment on December 2, 1865, all remaining African American slaves became free. Although the degree of true freedom actually experienced by African Americans remained severely limited by racial prejudice, slavery as an institution had been abolished forever.

The chair used by General Robert E. Lee and the chair and table used by General Ulysses S. Grant to sign the terms of surrender at Appomattox Court House, April 9, 1865. NMAH

General Lee sat in the caned arm chair at left when he signed the terms of surrender. General E. W. Whitaker acquired it, and it remained in his possession until November 3, 1871. he then presented the chair to the relief fund of the Nathaniel Lyon Post, Grand Army of the Republic, to be awarded to the person selling the most tickets for a benefit performance. Captain Patrick O'Farrell sold ninety-six tickets and became the new owner of the chair. His widow, Bridget E. O'Farrell, donated the chair to the national collections in 1915.

General Grant used this small spool-turned table to sign the document setting forth the surrender terms. After the signing, Lieutenant General Philip H. Sheridan, U.S. Army, pre- sented the table to Elizabeth B. Custer, the wife of Major General George A. Custer. In 1912 Mrs. Custer lent the table to the National Museum. In 1936, according to the terms of her will, the loan became a bequest and has remained in the national collections since then.

The inscription on the chair at right reads: "This is the chair in which

Genl. U.S. Grant sat when he signed the Articles of Capitulation resulting in the surrender of the Confederate Army by Genl. R.E. Lee at Appomattox Court House, Virginia, April 9th, 1865."

General Henry Capehart of the U.S. Volunteers acquired this chair. In 1893 he gave it to General Wilmon W. Blackmar, who left it in his will to the national collections.

For most of his adult life, Robert E. Lee (1807–70) was an officer in the United States Army. He initially disapproved of the South's secession from the Union as a solution to regional political disputes. But when his native Virginia left the Union to join the Confederacy in April 1861, he concluded that he had no choice but to join the new breakaway nation.

Lee's decision provided the South with one of its most important human assets. As commander of the Army of Northern Virginia from May 1862 until the end of the war, Lee demonstrated an extraordinary capacity for drawing the best from his soldiers. Moreover, his brilliance as a strategist was unri-

valed. It was largely due to him that the South was able to hold out for as long as it did against the North's substantially larger and far better supplied army.

When Lee sat for this bust in 1870, he seemed to sense that he was dying, for he told the sculptor Edward Valentine (1838–1930) that he had better not delay his work. Within four months of the sculpture's completion, Lee was dead, and Valentine modeled a recumbent likeness of Lee for the general's mausoleum.

Sculpture of Robert E. Lee, by Edward Valentine, 1870, bronze. NPG

Ulysses S. Grant and His 26 Generals, by Ole Peter Hansen Balling, about 1865, oil on canvas. NPG

By mid-1864, it was clear that the Union armies would soon subdue the Confederacy. Anticipating this victory, the Norwegian-born artist Ole Peter Hansen Balling (1823–1906) began planning a large panoramic canvas depicting the triumphant commander of the northern army, Ulysses S. Grant (1822–85), riding with members of his staff.

The figures in the picture are *(left to right):* Thomas Casimir Devin, George Custer, Hugh Kilpatrick, William Emory, Philip Sheridan, James McPherson, George Crook, Wesley Merritt, George Thomas, Gouverneur Warren, George Meade, John Parke, William Sherman, John Logan, Ulysses Grant, Ambrose Burnside, Joseph Hooker, Winfield Scott Hancock, John Rawlins, Edward Ord, Francis Preston Blair, Alfred Howe Terry, Henry Slocum, Jefferson Columbus Davis, Oliver Howard, John Schofield, and Joseph Mower.

A Celebration of Community

A community is the immediate frame of reference for our everyday lives. Communities are the places we live, the people we know, the institutions we create, and the leaders we follow. They are the forums in which we experience aspects of our culture on the most personal level. Within communities, we celebrate rites of passage, observe sacred and festive ceremonies, and remember our past together.

By providing the framework in which we learn, work, and play, communities are integral components of our identities. A community's vitality comes from the diversity of its people, the objects and graphic materials they create, and the memories they share. The Smithsonian's collections document the histories and vibrancy of communities and help us remember their importance in our lives.

REMEMBRANCES OF EVERYDAY LIFE

The Smithsonian houses the memorabilia of presidents, celebrities, sports heroes, renowned scientists, and acclaimed artists. But the majority of the Smithsonian's objects were once the possessions of ordinary people. The Smithsonian preserves such familiar things because the passage of time transforms the ordinary into the extraordinary. The tools, toys, and clothing that the Smithsonian collected as a matter of course more than a century ago are some of the same items we marvel at today. The everyday things that the Smithsonian continues to collect will become artifacts that will intrigue later generations and teach them about us.

These are the treasures of our own lives. They help us trace the persistence of our customs and ideals. They acquaint us with what is unfamiliar, and comfortably reaffirm what is familiar. In preserving these artifacts, we make ourselves more accessible to future generations.

These objects are part of a larger group of personal effects—including dolls, packets of old letters, photographs, old school books and cookbooks, record albums, clothing and shoes, souvenirs, and purses with the contents still in them—donated to the Anacostia Museum by the Griffiths family of Washington, D.C. Passed down from one generation to another, they became filled with meaning for their owners. They remain symbols of the personal stories, people, and places inhabiting their owners' memories.

The collection consists of items dating from the early 1900s through the 1960s. These keepsake boxes and old jewelry boxes contain the traces of daily life—from bus tokens and business cards to political buttons and holiday souvenirs. This 1950s television set was the first on the block, and neighbors used to gather at the Griffiths' home to watch it. The letters in some of the old purses and jewelry boxes record the employment, social activities, and family life of Delaphine Griffith who lived in Washington and often worked as a domestic in resort areas like Atlantic City, New Jersey. Subsequent letters trace the long struggle of her daughter, Jacqueline Griffith, to obtain federal employment in Washington.

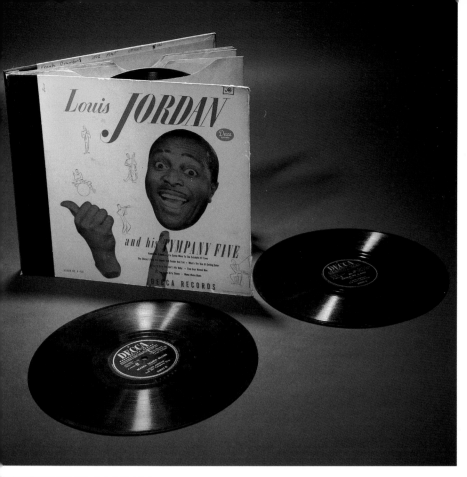

Griffiths family keepsakes
(from top left): record
album, *Louis Jordan and
His Tympany;* keepsake
box; television set; black
toddler doll in a child's
bent twig chair; and vinyl
jewelry box. AM

Beckley farm wagon, eastern United States, built about 1860, wood and iron (with reproduction cover). NMAH

Farm wagons were among the most common horse-drawn vehicles in the United States in the 19th and early 20th centuries. Henry Beckley (1827-1912), a master blacksmith in St. Clairsville, Pennsylvania, built this wagon about 1860, and it remained in service for eighty-five years. For part of that period, the Dibert family of Bedford County, Pennsylvania, used it to carry farm produce to the town of Bedford and to take feed and other supplies back to their farm.

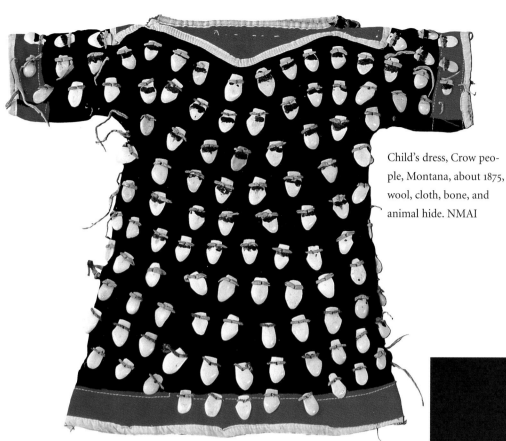

Child's dress, Crow people, Montana, about 1875, wool, cloth, bone, and animal hide. NMAI

Young woman's dress, Chinese American, New York City, mid-1930s, satin. NMAH

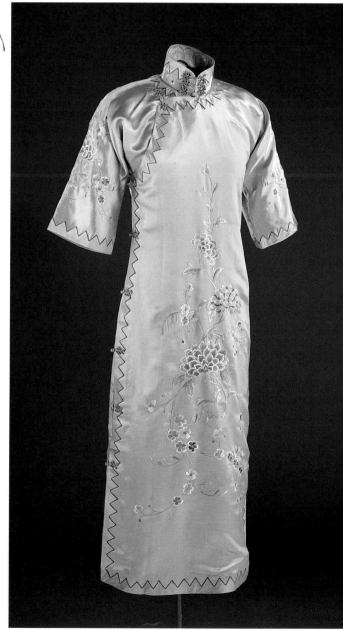

The maker of this child's dress, fashioned from red and blue wool cloth, decorated it lavishly with carved replicas of elk teeth. Because the Crow used only the elk's two upper canines for decoration, they were rare and costly. A man had to be a good hunter to acquire a large number. When real teeth were not available, the Crow crafted substitutes, such as the ones on this dress, with skill and care.

For the Crow, elk teeth symbolized love and long life, so they often presented them (or replicas) as gifts when a child was born. This dress speaks to us of the love that the maker felt for the child who wore it.

RIGHT: Virginia Lee wore this dress when she was a young woman living in New York City's Chinatown during the mid-1930s. Beginning in 1891, her father, Lee B. Lok, owned and ran Quong Yen Shing and Company—a store that was practically a self-contained community center. It functioned as a mail-drop, a traditional herbal pharmacy, a place for exchanging Chinese and American currency, a dry-goods store, and a center for customers eager to catch up on com-munity news. It was the focal point of the local Chinese American com-munity, of which this dress is a poignant memento.

The dress is a tradi-tional Chinese style, made of peach-colored satin and decorated with mul-ticolored embroidery. It is a style that younger second-generation Chi-nese women like Virginia Lee wore to weddings, formal dinners, and holi-day celebrations. They retained the style to cele-brate their traditions, her-itage, and ethnic identity.

Man's shirt, Sans Arc
Sioux, western plains, late
19th century, deer hide,
glass beads, human hair,
and pigment. NMAI

Hiroshima Kazuo (b. 1915)—the last traveling basket maker serving the villagers of Hinokage and elsewhere on the island of Kyūshyū, Japan—made this basket in 1986. It is the product of a long tradition of basket making in rural Japan.

Villagers on the Gokase River still fill traps with fragrant bait—usually sweet-smelling barley or boiled ocean-fish bones—to catch dace, which feed on the bottom of the river. Fishermen lower the traps into place to catch them while they feed. The trap's rectangular mouth is fitted with a flexible gate made of bamboo strips to prevent the fish from swimming out. Small dace are served as *sashimi.* Large ones are broiled and then simmered in flavored sauce.

RIGHT: In the world of Native Americans living on the Plains during the 19th century, most peoples were migratory, following their "staff of life"—the buffalo. Their artwork had to be portable to accommodate their constant movements. As a result, it often became incorporated into everyday, usable items—even shirts.

Among the Sioux, the *Wicasa* ("Shirt Wearer") was a man selected by the people to serve as a highly respected leader. They expected him to exemplify the virtues of bravery, generosity, and wisdom. A *Wicasa* shirt was decorated with locks of human hair, symbolic of the leader's responsibility for all his people. Craftsmen decorated this shirt with beaded strips and painted it blue and yellow with dots of mercury vermilion.

Fishtrap basket, made by Hiroshima Kazuo, Japan, 1986. NMNH

Asante artists carve small, single wooden figures that women tuck into the backs of their skirts. This double figure (one side shown here) seated on a ceremonial stool is unusual and was probably kept in a shrine. The Asante believe that the figures ensure fertility, as well as the health and beauty of future children. In Asante society, women especially desire female offspring who will perpetuate the family line.

The bodies of these figures are usually cylin-drical. The exaggerated, flat, disklike head, high oval forehead, and ringed neck are conventions used by the sculptor to embody Asante ideals of beauty. The facial features are small and delicately carved. Some figures have patterned scars on the face and body and wear beads.

Double figure (akua'ba), Asante peoples, Ghana, early 20th century, wood, glass, and beads. NMAfA

Sam Olson hewed this 12-foot-long dog sled from hickory in 1922. Under contract to the U.S. Postal Service, Charlie Biederman used it to deliver mail over the 340-mile route between Eagle and Circle, Alaska, until 1938. Six dogs pulled the sled. Mail had been carried by dog sled between Eagle and Circle since the first post offices were established there in the late 1880s.

Dog sleds were once commonly used to carry mail in Alaska, especially when boats were rendered useless by the winter cold that froze lakes and rivers. Mail was so highly valued by Alaskan communities that people treated the dog teams and drivers like royalty. At roadhouses the drivers would be given the best chair for dinner, the nicest bunk at bedtime, and the first batch of hotcakes in the morning. In addition, the lead dog was allowed to sleep under a driver's bed without the slightest complaint from other travelers.

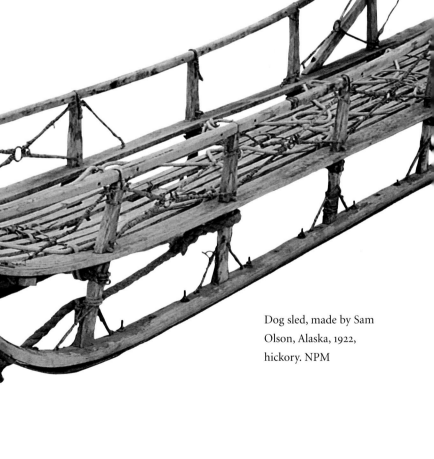

Dog sled, made by Sam Olson, Alaska, 1922, hickory. NPM

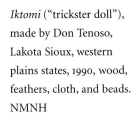

Iktomi ("trickster doll"), made by Don Tenoso, Lakota Sioux, western plains states, 1990, wood, feathers, cloth, and beads. NMNH

Don Tenoso (b. 1960) made this stuffed hide puppet with fully articulated joints to accompany storytelling at locations throughout the United States, including at the Smithsonian Institution. Inspired by puppets from Japan and southeast Asia, he crafted a puppet that could clasp the objects he made for it—including a gourd rattle, a shield, a drum, a feather fan, a coup stick, and a knife. He crafted them in order to teach children about 19th-century Lakota culture, but the objects also refer to attributes possessed by the traditional character represented by the doll in Lakota folktales.

The *Iktomi* is a trickster character who appears in tales as a spider or a coyote. The puppet wears a coyote robe and has a mask that he wears when he teaches people through deception. The piece exploits the humor inherent in trickster figures to address the tensions of being Lakota in the modern United States. It is also a striking example of cross-cultural fertilization, since puppets were unknown in traditional Lakota culture.

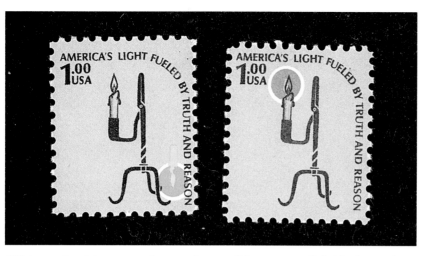

CIA inverted rush lamp stamp and correct rush lamp stamp, U.S. Postal Service, 1979. NPM

ABOVE: As part of the 1979 *Americana* series, the Bureau of Engraving and Printing designed a new stamp illustrated with a rush lamp and candleholder, a colonial illuminating device. A press printed one pane with the candleholder inverted. The bureau usually ferrets out these rare errors quickly and prevents them from reaching the public. When stamps with major mistakes reach the public, collectors consider them very valuable.

On March 27, 1986, employees from the Central Intelligence Agency purchased a partial pane of ninety-five inverted stamps from a McLean, Virginia, post office with government funds. The purchasers must have noticed the error immediately, for they did not use them on agency mail. They removed nine stamps from the top rows of the pane and retained those as souvenirs. They contacted Jaques C. Schiff, Jr., a prominent New Jersey stamp dealer specializing in stamp errors, and sold him the remainder. Schiff subsequently notified both the Bureau of Engraving and Printing and the postal service.

The CIA launched an internal investigation and identified the nine culprits. The agency interrogated the employees and ordered them to return the stamps or be fired. One person claimed he had lost his stamp and was believed; four refused and were fired; four returned theirs and retained their positions. The CIA turned the stamps over to the Smithsonian's National Philatelic Collection in 1990.

RIGHT: In the early 1930s, it became Postmaster General James A. Farley's practice to give a few special imperforate sheets of new stamps to friends. When this stamp came off the press on April 13, 1934, Farley gave one to Franklin Roosevelt, one to Eleanor Roosevelt, one to Secretary of the Interior Harold L. Ickes, one to the president's secretary Louis M. Howe, and the one shown here to his children.

Farley never intended these imperforate sheets to be sold to the public. But a collector in Norfolk, Virginia, obtained one sheet autographed by Farley on May 18, 1934. Believing that other collectors would pay a high price for it, he offered it to one dealer for $20,000—a sizable increase over its $6 face value. Philatelic societies called upon President Roosevelt, a fellow stamp collector, to stop the distribution of these sheets, since Farley's practice smacked of favoritism. Under such pressure, the post office agreed to sell imperforate sheets at face value. They became known as Farley's Follies.

Farley Follies sheet of stamps, signed by President Franklin D. Roosevelt, U.S. Postal Service, 1934. NPM

COMMUNITY LEADERSHIP

Throughout history, people have found leaders in educators, military commanders, statesmen, religious figures, civil rights advocates, authors, and orators. We admire these leaders—past and present—for their strong character, their experience, their moral vision, or their individual talent. We hold their staunch convictions and sense of social responsibility in high regard. Their determination, insight, and skill command our loyalty and respect. We take direction from our leaders, aspire to their visions, and even seek to emulate aspects of their lives.

Portrait of Mary McLeod Bethune, by Betsy Graves Reyneau, 1943–44, oil on canvas. NPG

Mary McLeod Bethune (1875–1955) believed that education represented the best route out of poverty for African Americans. In 1904, with a fund of $1.50, she established a normal-industrial school for girls in Daytona Beach, Florida. Within a decade, the enterprise was thriving.

It eventually became the fully accredited institution now known as Bethune-Cookman College.

Perhaps Bethune's greatest achievements grew out of her membership in the New Deal's unofficial "black cabinet," which aimed to move the government toward curbing racial discrimination in American life. Among the fruits of her efforts was Roosevelt's 1941 presidential order requiring equal consideration for African American job-seekers in federal employment and in defense industries.

Bethune's portrait is part of a series created by Betsy Graves Reyneau to call attention to noted black leaders' contributions to American life. Hanging in the background of the portrait is a picture of Faith Hall, the first major building erected at Bethune-Cookman College. When Betsy Graves Reyneau (1888–1964) painted the portrait, Bethune had no need for the cane she held. Instead, she regarded it as a stage prop that, as she put it, gave her "swank."

Jacket owned by Cesar Chavez. NMAH

BELOW: This altar—one of the most important icons of the early Chicano civil rights movement—served in a Catholic mass held in the fields near Delano, California, on March 10, 1968. The bishop of Los Angeles celebrated the mass, and several dignitaries and statesmen, including Senator Robert F. Kennedy, attended. The mass marked a significant moment in the history of the United Farm Workers Union and the Chicano civil rights movement by commemo-rating the end of a twenty-three-day fast by Cesar Chavez.

Symbolic imagery on the altar, created by Emanuel Martinez (b. 1947), includes an eagle, the sun, a peace symbol, and the Catholic crucifix. Four clasped hands, representing different races, express the theme of harmony in cosmic, social, and earthly forces. Representatives of the races harvest grapes in idealized harmony.

ABOVE: Cesar Chavez (1927–93) inspired the United States public to demand just compensation for some of the poorest of its laborers. A second-generation Mexican American and a migrant worker since childhood, he dedicated his life to improving the lot of his fellow workers. Inspired by the wisdom of Gandhi and Martin Luther King, Jr., Chavez pledged himself to the principle of nonviolent resistance.

For decades reformers' and labor leaders' attempts to organize farm workers in the United States had met with failure. It was not until 1962, when Cesar Chavez began organizing the predominantly Latino-Californian migrant farm workers with no outside financial support, that the first effective union was established. Through community organizing, strikes, marches, boycotts, and fasts, this small, dedicated union began to win better working conditions for farm workers. The union continues to fight an uphill battle to provide farm workers with the benefits most Americans believe working people deserve—a safe work place and a decent wage.

Farm worker's altar, by Emanuel Martinez, 1967, acrylic on mahogany and plywood. NMAA

Photograph of William Edward Burghardt Du Bois, by Carl Van Vechten, 1946 photogravure, 1983 print. NPG

W. E. B. Du Bois (1868–1963), who in 1895 became the first African American to earn a Ph.D. from Harvard, was widely respected for his sociological and historical studies of the African American community. He was better known, though, as a leading force in the early black civil rights movements. In 1905, rejecting those who said that equality for his people could come only gradually, Du Bois became a founder of the Niagara Movement, which called for an immediate end to racial discrimination. Four years later, he helped establish the National Association for the Advancement of Colored People and for twenty-five years served as the outspoken editor of its magazine, the *Crisis*.

Increasingly skeptical of his country's ability to stop racism and accused of disloyalty as a result of his Communist sympathies, Du Bois eventually felt thoroughly alienated from America. In 1962 he immigrated to Ghana in the hope of reviving "an ancient African communism" based on black spiritual unity. He died within the year. Although he did not fulfill his dream in Africa, he remains one of the most important African American leaders of this century.

The maker of Du Bois's portrait, writer-photographer Carl Van Vechten (1880–1964), was well known for his efforts to introduce white Americans to the work of African American artists and writers. He photographed Du Bois against this swirling backdrop in order to suggest his subject's electric energy.

Keokuk on Horseback, by George Catlin, 1835, oil on canvas. NMAA

According to the notes and letters of portraitist and preservationist George Catlin (1796–1872), Keokuk (The Watchful Fox) was a great warrior and diplomat of his people, the Sauk and Fox. Keokuk (about 1780–1848) traveled from his western homeland in present-day Oklahoma to Washington, D.C., to make speeches on behalf of his people. He sought to protect their rights while they negotiated with the government over the sale of native lands. In 1804 the Sauk and Fox had been duped into signing a treaty that required their removal from their original homelands around the Great Lakes to the arid lands of northwestern Oklahoma. Keokuk wished to prevent a similar incident from occurring again, but his speeches had little influence in Washington.

Catlin's equestrian portrait—with all the strength and symbolism of a Baroque monument—shows a commanding figure dressed in the trappings of a great warrior, leader, and statesman. Catlin believed that Native Americans and their culture were on the brink of extinction, as did many others of the period.

In early 1777 the Marquis de Lafayette (1757–1834) signed an agreement with Britain's rebelling colonies to serve in their armies without compensation. He was motivated partly by his native France's deep-rooted hatred of England and partly by sympathy for the political ideals of the American cause. By midsummer, he had joined Washington's staff and eventually became one of the American Revolution's most brilliant and beloved soldiers. In late 1781 he assured himself a place of preeminence in the war's pantheon of heroes by helping to corner the British forces at Yorktown, paving the way for their surrender to General Washington on October 19.

In 1824 Lafayette returned to the United States for a year-long tour. Everywhere he went, he encountered crowds eager to meet the Frenchman who had helped forge their nation. His visit yielded many portraits, including a full-length one by the European artist Ary Sheffer. The likeness shown here was derived from that picture and is probably the work of the Kentucky painter Matthew Jouett (1788–1827).

Portrait of the Marquis de Lafayette, probably by Matthew Harris Jouett after Ary Sheffer, about 1825, oil on canvas. NPG

King Kamehameha IV.

Photograph of Kamehameha III, by Henry L. Chase, about 1870, albumen silver print after an 1850 daguerreotype. NPG

From 1810 to 1893, the islands of Hawaii were a united kingdom governed by a single monarchy. During that period, one of the most effective and revered figures to occupy the throne was Kamehameha III

(1814–54). Coming to power in 1825, he ruled for nearly thirty years. Under his rule Hawaii experienced considerable economic growth and prosperity. The reign of Kamehameha III saw the significant expansion of public education, the adoption of Hawaii's first penal code, and the implementation of a constitution patterned largely on those of American state governments.

Henry Chase (1831–1901) worked as a

photographer in Hawaii between 1862 and 1901 and made this picture long after Kamehameha III had died. He copied it from an image taken by another photographer about 1850.

Photograph of Kamehameha IV, by Henry L. Chase, about 1862, albumen silver print. NPG

King of the Hawaiian Islands from 1854 to 1863, Kamehameha IV (1834–63) feared that strong American economic influence in his kingdom would ultimately lead to its annexation by the United States. As a result, the policies of his reign were largely shaped by his desire to prevent such an occurrence.

Based in Honolulu, Henry Chase photographed many of Hawaii's prominent late-19th-century residents.

For the native peoples of the northwest coast, masks make the supernatural world visible. When people wear masks, they become like the spirits or mythical beings they represent. Masked dancers dramatize the encounters of ancestral heroes with supernatural creatures, and demonstrate the prestige of their families. The right to use these masks remains inherited in most northwest coast groups. Shamans use other masks representing spirit powers to treat illness.

Northwest Coast mask makers are professional artists, skilled in the imaginative rendering of mythical creatures. A Bella Coola sculptor in British Columbia, Canada, made this human raven mask. Among the supernatural beings represented by Bella Coola mask-makers are many combinations of birds, other animals, and humans. In Bella Coola myths, animals could assume human form, and this mask probably represents that possibility. The raven is an important character in these myths as a trickster figure combining mischief and benevolence.

Human raven mask, Bella Coola people, Pacific northwest coast, mid-19th century, wood and pigment. NMNH

Among the Yaure, masks often combine human and animal characteristics and are believed to possess extraordinary powers. Representing spirits who inhabit the realm of nature, they are sometimes called into villages during rites of passage, when young men wear them during daytime or nocturnal dances. People also use masks during funerary ceremonies, for they allow the spirits of deceased people to join their ancestors in the afterlife. When such ceremonies end, the Yaure return the masks to the sacred grove outside the village, and life returns to normal.

Mask, Yaure peoples, Côte d'Ivoire, early 20th century, wood and pigment. NMAfA

Reliquary guardian figure
(bwiti), Hongwe peoples,
Gabon, early 20th century,
wood, copper, and brass.
NMAfA

Among the Hongwe peoples of Gabon, art performed one paramount function—the attraction and containment of protective spirits to help the living maintain social order, attain leadership, and assure good fortune. The Hongwe expected spirits to work in combination with the magical power of family relics—most often skulls—on behalf of the living. They placed the remains of deceased family members in containers or reliquaries. Wooden images, covered with brass strips, stood guard over the sacred relics.

The Hongwe held brass, a trade item, in especially highly esteem. They used it to decorate images representing protective spirits and to make objects for personal adornment.

Ghost Dance dress,
Arapaho peoples, central
plains states, about 1890.

OPPOSITE: The Ghost Dance was a religious movement that began in the 1880s and spread rapidly among the Plains peoples. It was based on a vision by a Paiute Prophet, Wovoka. He had proclaimed that a new age would dawn for Native Americans, relieving the near-destruction of their culture by the white man. Wovoka said that if the people were good and sang certain songs, danced, and prayed, then their ancestors would return, the buffalo would return, and the white man would disappear. The movement was strictly nonviolent and was characterized by peoples' participation in ecstatic dances and communal ceremonies. In 1890 the movement came to a bloody end when U.S. soldiers attacked a group of worshipers at Wounded Knee and killed about 250 of them, including Sitting Bull.

Believers wore clothing decorated with symbols of the sun, the moon, and stars, as well as animals with special powers. This Arapaho dress is painted with the stars and a crescent moon, the turtle that brought soil for the creation of the world, and birds that act as messengers to the spirit world.

For Native Americans in the northwest, totem poles either serve as mortuary poles or proclaim the status of a clan. The figures carved onto the poles symbolize the mythological history of a clan and the rights and privileges it enjoys on account of its history. On this pole the figures represent, from top to bottom, a man, a bear, and a frog. They signify the specific rights and privileges of the family that erected the pole near its residence in southeastern Alaska.

Totem Pole, probably Tlingit peoples, Pacific northwest, mid-19th century, wood and pigment. NMNH

La Divina Pastora, by José Aragon, New Mexico, about 1825, wood and pigment. NMAH

ABOVE: This panel by José Aragon (active 1825–35) depicts the Virgin as "the divine shepherdess." *Retablo* is the Spanish term New Mexican Hispanics use to refer to images of saints painted on flat wooden panels. The oldest documented New Mexican *retablos* date to the 1780s. Some still remain in Catholic homes, and they are used during a family's private devotions. These images permit worshipers to maintain close spiritual contact with God by seeking the intercession of the saints and the Virgin Mary.

LEFT: Puerto Rican Catholics refer to this image of the Virgin Mary as "Our Lady of Montserrat." The image is inspired by a legend popular in northeast Spain, especially in the Catalan-speaking region of the Pyrenees. In the small village of Hormigüeros devotees transformed the original legend into a local miracle story. According to their version, commemorated by this painted sculpture *(imagen de bulto),* the Virgin Mary miraculously appeared to save a humble rural man *(jibaro)* whose life was threatened by a charging bull.

Milagro de la Virgen de Hormigüeros ("Miracle of the Virgin of Hormigüeros"), Puerto Rico, about 1890, wood and pigment. NMAH

Ritual instrument *(cong)*,
China, about 2500 B.C.,
jade. AMSG

The shapes of most
Chinese ritual jades were
derived from late Neo-
lithic stone implements.
But the *cong* are a striking exception. The dimen-
sions and proportions of
cong vary considerably,
though the essential form
remains the same and all
are made of jade.

It is probable that rit-
ual usage initially dictat-
ed the form of the *cong*.
But their exact function
or significance remains
uncertain. *Cong* have
been found in graves
arranged around the
corpse, suggesting they
held protective powers
that could be desirable to
the dead in the afterlife.

Quilt appliquéd with fruit and flowers, made by Mary Carpenter Pickering, Ohio, mid-19th century, cotton fabric. NMAH

Mary Carpenter Pickering (1831–1900) worked on this quilt when her friend John Bruce Bell accompanied a wagon train to the Oregon Territory. He left St. Clairsville, Ohio, in 1850 and returned eight years later. They were married September 3, 1861. Shortly thereafter, Bell joined the Union Army to serve in the Civil War. John and Mary Bell moved to Keokuk County, Iowa, in 1864 and had nine children. This quilt is said to have won a blue ribbon at the Ohio State Fair in the early 1850s.

In American culture, quilts are often passed down through the generations of a family, becoming treasures that commemorate their makers. Mary Pickering's quilt and its history have been cherished by three generations of her family. A granddaughter relates that Mary made the appliquéd top at age 13, not returning to it until age 19 to add the elaborate quilting and stuffed work.

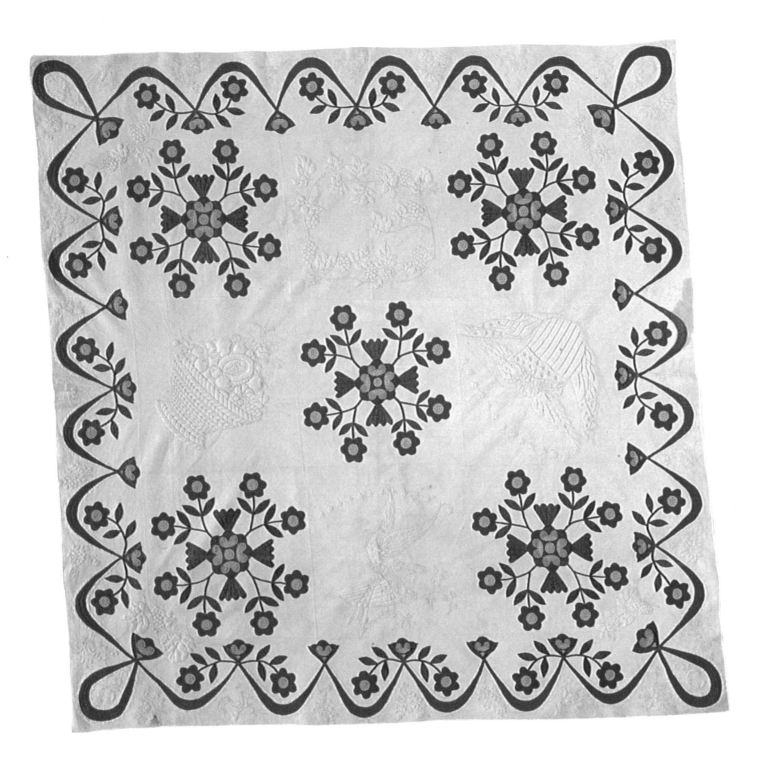

Quilt, United States,
mid-19th century, cotton
fabric. NMAH

The designer and maker of this intricate quilt is unknown, but the painstaking care that the maker took to create this heirloom is obvious. She appliquéd the center and four corner blocks with a large Rose of Sharon variation. The remaining four blocks have large quilted-and-stuffed motifs: an eagle with shield and flags, an eagle with arrows and olive branch, a grapevine, and a basket of fruit. The appliquéd swags and roses of the border are interspersed with thirty-six small quilted-and-stuffed motifs—birds on branches, flowers, and grapes. The background is closely quilted with diagonal lines.

Bear-claw necklace (with trailer at left), Mesquakie peoples, central plains states, about 1860, grizzly bear claws, otter pelt, glass beads, and ribbon. NMAI

The Mesquakie, as well as other Prairie and Plains warriors, place a high value on bear-claw necklaces. They are signs of bravery and, consequently, stature. Although several tribes made them, Mesquakie and Sauk necklaces were widely admired and, in fact, prized by various groups because of the skill with which they were made.

Typically, individual bear claws were connected by large, decorative glass beads and worn around the neck. A long, beautifully ornamented otter-pelt trailer hung from the back. This particularly fine necklace has a trailer decorated with glass seed beads and silk ribbon.

Feathered crown, Kaapor
(Urubu) peoples, Brazil,
about 1962, cotton cordage
and feathers of yellow
japo ararajuba, scarlet
macaw, and black *mutum*.
NMAI

The Kaapor, who live in
the lush tropical forests
of northeastern Brazil,
are well known for their
spectacular feather orna-
ments. This man's crown
(akangatar) is composed
of three elements—a cot-
ton band, feather strings,
and feather pendants.
When worn, the head-
dress opens over the eyes
like a sun visor, and the
feather pendants fall over
the temples. Men usually
wear these elaborate head
ornaments for ceremo-
nial occasions.

Eagle feather war bonnet, Pawnee peoples, central plains states, 1939, golden eagle feathers, wool cloth, and glass beads. NMAI

The war bonnet, with its long trailer of feathers, has become the quintessential symbol of honor and accomplishment among Plains tribes. In recent years, other Native American peoples have adopted it as well. The preferred feathers—and the ones used in this war bonnet—are from the tail of the golden eagle. Although not as precious, other feathers are often used, including those of the grouse, turkey, pheasant, and bald eagle. This Pawnee war bonnet was given to General Robert Lee Bullard in 1939 on the occasion of his being made an honorary chief of the Pawnee tribe.

Feather war bonnet, Comanche peoples, central plains states, about 1900, parrot feathers, cloth, glass beads, and animal horn. NMAI

This unusual and colorful Comanche war bonnet is made of parrot feathers rather than the more usual eagle feathers. Collected in Oklahoma in 1914, it shows Native Americans' use of exotic materials in the creation of a traditional piece of regalia. The Comanches, like other Native American peoples, permit only brave, honorable, and respected men to wear the war bonnet.

American Inventors and Inventions

Since 1790 the United States Patent Office has granted more than 6 million patents. The number of patents issued increased dramatically during the 19th century, stimulated by and further stimulating the American industrial revolution. The decade ending in 1800 saw the issuance of only 306 patents. In contrast, the decade ending in 1860 saw 28,000 issued. The middle and late 19th century was a golden age for American invention. The new technology envisioned by our inventors has changed the face of the United States—improving our standard of living and linking us across physical and cultural divides.

The Smithsonian Institution cares for thousands of the models that inventors were required to submit with their patent applications before 1880. These models represent not only the most famous inventions that changed America but also many lesser-known ones that represent the small technical changes that allowed the development of more significant technologies.

"Box" telephone, invented by Alexander Graham Bell, 1876. NMAH

While Alexander Graham Bell (1847–1922) was experimenting with telegraph instruments in the early 1870s, he realized that it might be possible to transmit the human voice over a wire by using electricity. By March 1876 he managed to make a transmission, but the sound was very faint.

He improved the results with a series of experiments over the next few months, including a critical test with this instrument on November 26. That day he transmitted sound clearly over a wire between Cambridge and Salem, Massachusetts. This design, used for both the transmitter and the receiver, became standard for the commercial instruments introduced in 1877.

Patent model for a sugar
evaporation system,
invented by Norbert
Rillieux, 1843. AM

Norbert Rillieux
(1806–94), an African
American inventor from
New Orleans, patented
his multiple-effect vacu-
um evaporation system
in 1843. He designed it to
evaporate the liquid part
of sugar cane juice more
efficiently, more safely,
and less expensively than
the open-kettle system
then in use.

Rillieux was not able
to persuade local sugar
cane plantation owners
to invest in his machin-
ery until several years
after he had patented it.
But its superiority to the
old open-kettle system
became almost immedi-
ately apparent after the
device had begun to be
used widely. It proved so
efficient that planters

could recover the cost of
the machinery with the
extra profits they realized
from the first crop of
sugar cane processed
under the new method.

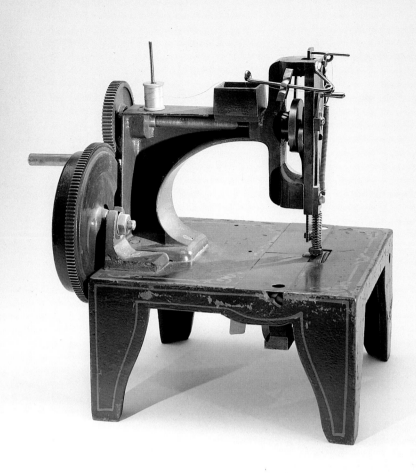

Sewing machine patent model, patented May 30, 1853, patent number 10975, invented by Isaac M. Singer. NMAH

As early as the mid-18th century, European inventors sought to overcome the technical problems of mechanical sewing. Often they tried to mimic the motions used in hand sewing, but without success. In the early 19th century, some American inventors also looked for ways to mechanize sewing by simulating the motions of sewing by hand. Others, however, took a more innovative approach. Elias Howe, Jr., patented his first sewing machine in 1846. It incorporated some, but not all, of the elements of a successful machine.

Isaac Merritt Singer (1811–75), the most flamboyant of the sewing machine inventors, had sharpened his skills as an actor, mechanic, cabinet maker, and inventor. Unable to market his first invention—an improved type-carving machine—he concentrated on improving the defective model of an already existing sewing machine.

Success followed quickly. For his first patent model in 1851, he submitted one of his commercial sewing machines. This model, Singer's 5th, is also a commercial machine. The specific patent claims allowed were for the methods of feeding the cloth, regulating the tension on the needle thread, and lubricating the needle thread so that leather could be sewn. The development of practical sewing machines contributed to the expansion of the ready-made clothing industry. By the 1920s inexpensive, ready-made clothing was widely available.

Altair computer, 1975. NMAH

In recent years it has become clear that the invention of the personal computer is having an effect on our lives equal to, if not greater than, the invention of the telegraph, telephone, or electric light. The Altair was the most popular early personal computer. Instructions for building it first appeared in the January 1975 issue of *Popular Electronics*. An early Altair kit cost $397 and a fully assembled machine $498.

The Altair was programmed by flipping the switches on the front panel. Its output was simply a pattern of lights. Communications, word processing, and other applications required additional components. Many early microcomputer companies got their start making circuit boards for the Altair. It spawned several software companies, most notably Microsoft.

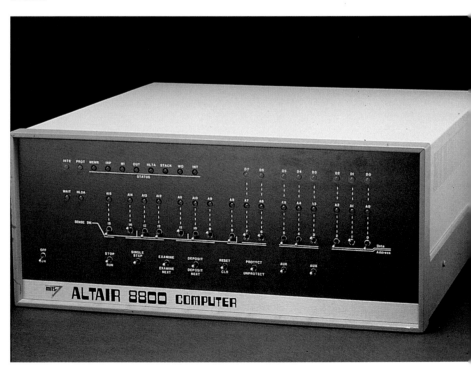

Photograph of Jonas Salk,
1963, by Philippe
Halsman, gelatin silver
print. NPG

For years polio—with its power to paralyze and kill—numbered among the most dreaded contagious diseases. Because children were its most vulnerable victims, the mere mention of a possible outbreak was enough to generate widespread panic. By the early 1950s, however, hope for the conquest of polio began to mount in the wake of promising new efforts to control the disease.

Among those leading the assault on the polio virus was Jonas Salk (1914–95), founder of the University of Pittsburgh's Research Laboratory. In 1954 Salk and his Pittsburgh associates began the human testing of what proved to be the first truly effective antipolio vaccine. Within another few years, outbreaks of the terrible disease were fast becoming a thing of the past.

Philippe Halsman took this picture of Salk at the site chosen in San Diego, California, for the Salk Institute for Biological Studies.

American Pastimes

American popular culture includes a variety of experiences that entertain and delight vast audiences. A wide variety of ethnic and regional traditions, as well as social history, have shaped the forms American entertainment has acquired. Our pastimes have become as diverse as the people who created them. American literature, music, film, television, and athletic events continually evolve as new generations expand the boundaries established by those before. Popular culture unites us through our shared delight in the variety of amusements open to us.

The Smithsonian's Popular Culture collections contain many of the most famous and familiar objects preserved in the Institution. Their popularity reflects their role as mementos of the experiences we have enjoyed and shared.

AMERICAN WRITERS

Remembering the past and assessing the present through the prism of their own lives have long been concerns of American writers. Many have tended to cultivate a two-fold vision. These authors explore the tensions and contradictions they see in our complex societies, and they do so from a perspective that remains intensely personal, rooted in irreducible individual experience.

The Smithsonian preserves objects that give us avenues into writers' personal lives and the genesis of their literary visions. By examining them, we commemorate not only their works and lives but also many of the issues they sought to address.

Pearl Buck (1892–1973) was a prolific writer, and her long list of both fictional and nonfictional works treats many subjects. But her most memorable achievements are her chronicles of China, where she had grown up as the daughter of Presbyterian missionaries. In the early 1920s, following the completion of a number of short stories and articles on China, her literary ambitions grew. In 1930 she published her first novel, *East Wind: West Wind,* a study of the clash between the old and the new China. The success of that work was eclipsed the next year with the appearance of *The Good Earth,* Buck's sensitive portrayal of Chinese peasant society. In addition to becoming a best-seller and inspiring a Broadway play, this novel won a Pulitzer Prize. Over the next several years, Buck completed a number of other books about China. In 1938 she became the first American woman to be awarded the Nobel Prize in literature.

Made at about the time Buck was admitted to the American Academy of Arts and Letters, this photograph is the work of Clara Sipprell (1885–1975). A member of the pictorialist school of photography, Sipprell sought to create portraits that conveyed atmosphere and mood as well as likeness.

Photograph of Pearl Buck, by Clara Sipprell, about 1950, gelatin silver print. NPG

F. Scott Fitzgerald (1896–1940) named the self-indulgent 1920s "the Jazz Age," and his best-selling novel, *This Side of Paradise,* became one of the decade's first literary landmarks. But his most enduring achievement was *The Great Gatsby,* a meticulously crafted tale of failed love set against a background of careless luxury.

For *Gatsby* and much of his other work, Fitzgerald drew from his own marriage to the Alabama beauty Zelda Sayre. At the outset of their life together, they were often viewed as America's smartest—though somewhat errat-ic—literary couple. But as Fitzgerald succumbed to alcoholism and his wife to insanity, their life dissolved into tragedy. Fitzgerald's last complete novel, *Tender Is the Night,* is largely an exam-ination of what had gone wrong in their lives.

In 1935, when the Virginia artist David Silvette (b. 1909) suggest-ed to Fitzgerald at a party that he should sit for a portrait, Fitzgerald was suffering from an emo-tional breakdown. But he agreed to pose. When the painting was finished, Fitzgerald wrote to his editor, Maxwell Perkins: "I've had a swell portrait painted . . . and next time I come to New York I am going to spend a morning tearing out of your files all those preposterous masks with which you have been libeling me for the last decade."

Portrait of F. Scott Fitzgerald, by David Silvette, 1935, oil on canvas. NPG

African American writer Langston Hughes (1902–67) published his first poem before he left high school. In 1926, with the appearance of his volume of verse, *The Weary Blues,* he became a central figure in the cultural movement known as the Harlem Renaissance. Critics—blacks as well as whites—sometimes faulted the prolific and versatile Hughes for dwelling on the negative aspects of his race's experience in this country. But in much of his work, there is a humor and optimism that transcends the unpleasant realities he portrayed. "I am the darker brother," he once wrote, "They send me to eat in the Kitchen / When company comes. / But I laugh, / And eat well, / And grow strong."

The maker of this likeness was the writer, critic, and amateur photographer Carl Van Vechten. He was among the first members of America's white literary establishment to recognize the creative richness and cultural significance of Harlem Renaissance writers. Van Vechten played an important role in the publication of Hughes's *Weary Blues,* and he did much to bring it to the attention of other critics.

Photograph of Langston Hughes, by Carl Van Vechten, 1983 photogravure from 1939 negative. NPG

Posthumous portrait of
Mark Twain, by Frank
Edwin Larson, 1935, oil on
canvas. NPG

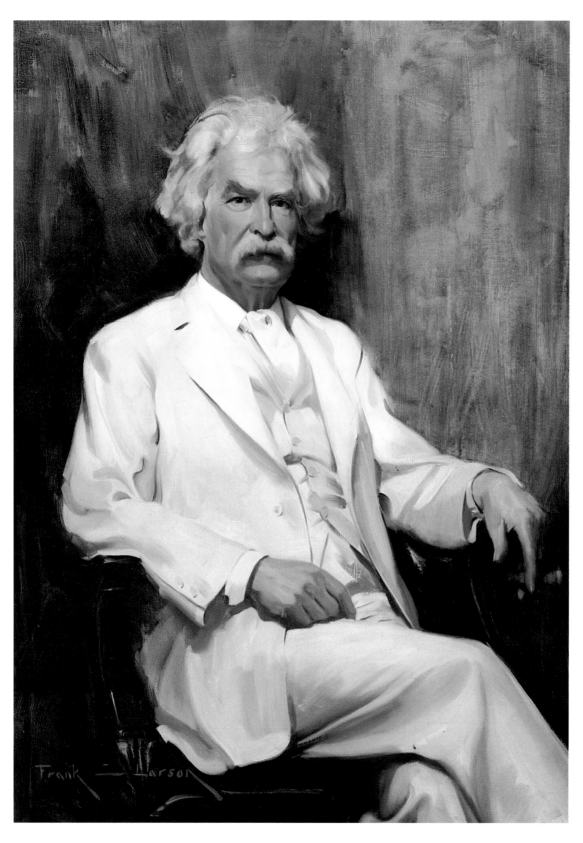

Using the pen name Mark Twain, Samuel Clemens (1835–1910) had become one of this country's favorite satiric writers by the early 1870s. But it was his publication of *The Adventures of Tom Sawyer* in 1876 and *The Adventures of Huckleberry Finn* in 1885 that assured him lasting preeminence in American letters. Inspired by his own boyhood in Hannibal, Missouri, Twain's two pre–Civil War tales of youth along the Mississippi have delighted readers for generations. Ernest Hemingway's assertion that "all modern American literature" began with *Huckleberry Finn* may be something of an overstatement, but there is no doubt Twain transformed the country's tradition of humorous colloquial narrative into high art.

Frank Edwin Larson (1895–1991) painted this portrait for the Mark Twain Centennial Exhibition at Hannibal, Missouri. He based it on a series of photographs taken in the early 1900s by New York photographer Frederick Bradley, Sr.

Photograph of Walt Whitman, by an unidentified photographer, possibly Thomas Eakins, 1979 platinum print from 1891 negative. NPG

When Walt Whitman (1819–92) published *Leaves of Grass* in 1855, Ralph Waldo Emerson saw the event as a sign that a poet capable of expressing this country's democratic spirit had at last appeared. To the author of this free-verse American hymn, Emerson wrote, "I greet you at the beginning of a great career." But Emerson's enthusiasm for the unorthodox verse

form and imagery of *Leaves of Grass* was not widely shared, and general recognition of Whitman's poetic achievements was slow in coming. By the time he sat for this photograph in the early 1890s, however, Whitman had come to be regarded as the most original of this country's poets. More important, he had become both the symbol of, and the spokesman for, the

democratic promise of America.

It was thought for many years that this photograph and a number of others taken at the same time were the work of the Philadelphia artist Thomas Eakins, who had painted Whitman's portrait in 1888. However, recent research indicates that this series of pictures might have been taken either by Eakins's student

Samuel Murray or by Sophia Williams, wife of the Philadelphia journalist Talcott Williams.

American Music

Musical instruments, original sheet music, and portraiture preserved in the Smithsonian remind us that American music flourishes within a wide variety of traditions drawn from our multicultural heritage. From our country's urban centers to its rural landscapes, the sounds of many musical sounds and styles fill our lives.

The patriotic marches of John Philip Sousa, the exacting structures of classical music, the power and emotion of the blues, the swinging tones of the big band era, the seductive rhythms of jazz, the joys and sorrows expressed in country music, and the hard-charging beat of rock'n'roll—all serve to unite us. Their rich variety communicates across generations, races, and languages, and serves to break down cultural barriers.

Jazz

Jazz grew out of African American culture as it developed in the southern United States during the nineteenth century. It became intertwined with many other musical traditions, including Hispanic and Euro-American styles.

Since its beginnings, jazz has thrived on improvisation and change. Its greatest musicians have extended the technical and emotional ranges of their instruments and created new musical styles like bebop. On the bandstand and concert stage, these inspired innovators have taken musical risks and created a legacy of enduring recordings. Jazz has influenced virtually every other style of twentieth-century American music. It has become recognized as one of our country's greatest cultural achievements.

Heritage: EKE, posthumous portrait of Duke Ellington, by his granddaughter, Gaye Ellington, 1985, acrylic on canvas. NMAH

Gaye Ellington (b. 1955) painted this portrait of her grandfather Duke Ellington to create a memorial that preserved her sense of the creative and loving legacy he had left her. Like her grandfather, she is a colorist. Her painting expresses light, color, warmth, radiance, love, dynamism, and even an air of improvisation similar to her grandfather's music.

Recently, she explained the reasons that led her to create this portrait, even though portraiture is not her usual subject matter: "Ever since my grandfather had died, many artists have done representations of him. They were what other people saw in my grandfather. When I looked at them, they didn't express what I thought of him, and it disturbed me. . . . A lot of the photographs of him were very serious. I'm not saying he was always happy. But he would turn around in a minute and smile."

Music manuscript written
by Edward Kennedy
"Duke" Ellington, about
1940. NMAH

Duke Ellington (1899–1974) wrote the multi-movement work *Black, Brown and Beige* to chronicle the history of blacks in America. It debuted at Carnegie Hall on January 23, 1943, to mixed reviews. Some hailed it as a masterpiece and considered it a classical composition. Others derided it as an overly ambitious and underdeveloped work. Ellington continued to entertain audiences for thirty more years, but he never performed *Black, Brown and Beige* in its entirety again.

The first movement, *Black,* portrays the forced immigration and enslavement of Africans to America between 1620 and the American Revolution. Ellington integrated into his composition the sounds of spirituals and the blues to express the slaves' suffering and their belief in a better life after death. This document, "Light," is one part of *Black* and unmistakably an Ellington original. The G clef resembles the written capital "E" in Ellington's signature. Ellington also characteristically omits the stems from flat notations in the score. Moreover, in Ellington scores like this one, the bandmembers' names or nicknames mark their parts rather than the instruments they played, showing that Ellington tailored his compositions to his individual bandmembers.

B-flat Trumpet & Case, Silver Flair Model, 1972, owned by Dizzy Gillespie. NMAH

OPPOSITE: Trumpeter, bandleader, and composer John Birks "Dizzy" Gillespie (1917–93) ranks as one of the greatest musical innovators of the 20th century. With Charlie Parker, he was one of the founders of the jazz style called bebop. Gillespie developed asymmetrical melodies, innovatively used Latin American rhythms and adventurous harmonies, and extended the technical range of the trumpet. His musical virtuosity, wit, charm, and impish good humor came to an end when he died on January 6, 1993.

The King Musical Instrument Company of Eastlake, Ohio, made this Silver Flair trumpet, which Gillespie played from 1972 until the early 1980s. It has an upturned bell, a design for which Gillespie was internationally known. In 1953 someone fell on Gillespie's trumpet and bent the bell. He discovered he liked the sound and had trumpets specially built in that shape. The trumpet's case carries stickers for performances in Germany and France. Gillespie played the instrument in uncounted performances at concert halls, night clubs, jazz festivals, and recording sessions, as well as on television.

Portrait of John Birks "Dizzy" Gillespie, by Marc Klionsky, 1988, oil on canvas. NPG

In the early 1940s the young jazz trumpet player Dizzy Gillespie began meeting with several other musicians in their off-hours at a New York nightclub to explore a new avenue of musical expression. The sessions included Thelonious Monk and Charlie Parker, and out of them came a new jazz form that Gillespie inadvertently christened bebop.

Initially, the new music offended some jazz traditionalists, but its infectious energy soon brought it into the mainstream. Gillespie emerged as the personification of bebop and eventually became the elder statesman of American jazz. Gillespie's prominence, however, rested as much on the virtuosity of his playing as it did on his role as an originator of a new music form. In the 1970s one critic proclaimed him "the world's greatest trumpet [player] in or out of jazz."

Trained in the realist tradition of Soviet art, Gillespie's Russian-born portraitist, Marc Klionsky (b. 1927), settled in the United States in 1974. During sittings for Gillespie's likeness, the artist and his subject talked about African culture. Klionsky included the masks flanking Gillespie as reminders of their amiable conversations.

Arturo Toscanini claimed
that contralto Marian
Anderson had a voice
that came along "once in
a hundred years." When
one of her music teachers
first heard her sing, her
talent moved him to
tears. Because she was
black, however, Ander-
son's prospects as a
singer in this country
were initially quite
limited. She experienced
most of her early profes-
sional triumphs in
Europe, but eventually
the magnitude of her tal-
ent won her broad recog-
nition in the United
States. When she began
touring regularly in this
country in 1935, she was
quickly acknowledged as
the world's greatest con-
tralto. By the time
Anderson retired in the
mid-1960s, she was
regarded as a national
treasure.

Painted for the
Harmon Foundation,
founded to promote a
more universal awareness
of African American
achievement, this por-
trait shows Anderson as
she appeared at her con-
cert on the steps of the
Lincoln Memorial.

Fur coat worn by Marian
Anderson. AM

Though not a civil rights
activist, Marian Anderson
(1897–1993) helped to
break down racial barri-
ers in the United States. In
1939 the Daughters of the
American Revolution
refused to allow the
acclaimed contralto to
perform at its Constitu-
tion Hall in Washington,
D.C., because of her race.
Widespread outrage and
the efforts of Eleanor
Roosevelt and Secretary of
the Interior Harold Ickes

resulted in Anderson's
famous open-air concert
at the nearby Lincoln
Memorial in Washington,
D. C., on Easter Sunday,
1939. She sang before
thousands of people while
wearing this coat.

That concert became
an eloquent protest
against segregation and
transformed Anderson
into a symbol of this
country's struggle for
greater racial tolerance.
That same year, the

National Association for
the Advancement of
Colored People awarded
Anderson the Spingarn
Medal for her achieve-
ments in music.

In 1956 *Fortune* commissioned seven artists to look at "the stridently packaged goods of 1956" and paint what they saw "in a morning's haul from the supermarket." Stuart Davis (1894–1964) did just that. *Int'l Surface No. 1* was one of several paintings to come out of his exercise in attaining a new perspective on everyday reality.

To a synthesis of words, geometric Cubist forms, and the acidic, hard-edged colors of modern French Fauves ("Wild Beasts"), Davis added the dynamism of his own urban vision. The rhythms of this painting, the clarity of its form, its billboard scale, and its solid areas of color are all unmistakably influenced by American popular culture, especially by jazz.

Int'l Surface No. 1, by Stuart Davis, 1960, oil on canvas. NMAA

Jitterbugs (I), by William
H. Johnson, 1940–41, oil
on plywood. NMAA

William Henry Johnson (1901–70) described himself as a cultured artist, and he struggled to create a synthesis between the different elements of his background—his humble South Carolina origins, his training in New York and Paris during the 1920s, and his experience in environments as different as Harlem and Scandinavia. He developed a balance between the cultured and the primitive that remains evident throughout the numerous paintings, drawings, and prints he created during his twenty-five-year career.

In the words of Richard Powell, "this painting belongs to a series depicting couples dancing the Jitterbug, celebrating an African American music and dance form extremely popular in 1940s New York. In *Jitterbugs (I),* one of the earliest of these paintings, Johnson makes no attempt at all to capture the frenetic, acrobatic pace of the dancers. Instead, he stops the action, and allows his viewers to dissect the subtle gestures of the dancers and note the latest fashions."

Jitterbugs (I), by William
H. Johnson, 1940–41, oil
on plywood. NMAA

POPULAR ENTERTAINMENT: COMMUNICATING AMERICAN CULTURE

One of the most influential forms of popular art in the 20th century, American movies reach millions of people around the world and help to shape perceptions of American life. The images fashioned by Hollywood have reflected the shifting moods of a nation composed of diverse populations and changing interests.

Building partially on the mass appeal of motion pictures, television has become the United States' most pervasive national medium. It delivers a rich mixture of news, sports, entertainment, and advertising to audiences throughout the country. Its programs constantly evolve in response to changes in our society's values and concerns, as well as the medium's own financial interests.

Sculpted head of Charles S. "Charlie" Chaplin, by Jo Davidson, 1925, bronze. NPG

When moviemaker Mack Sennett saw the English vaudeville actor Charlie Chaplin (1889–1977) on the New York stage in 1912, he knew that he had spotted a great talent. Within two years—playing a mustachioed, duck-footed tramp in one comedy after another—Chaplin was well on his way to becoming America's favorite comedian on the silver screen. By the 1920s, after forming United Artists with Mary Pickford, Douglas Fairbanks, and D. W. Griffith, Chaplin had begun directing and writing his own films. Among his most noted accomplishments were his satiric commentary on the machine age, *Modern Times,* and his biting portrayal of Adolf Hitler in *The Great Dictator.*

Chaplin agreed to sit for this bust by Jo Davidson (1883–1952) at a New York dinner given in his honor in 1924. The sculptor found Chaplin a "wonderfully stimulating companion." But his mobile features made him a difficult subject. "He would sit there and never move a muscle," Davidson wrote, "and yet his face was constantly changing. He would look gay or sad, wise or silly at will."

Of all the names from this country's frontier past, few are more familiar than that of "Buffalo Bill" Cody (1846–1917). Born in Iowa, Cody began his rise to fame as a rider for the Pony Express. By the early 1870s, he had earned a reputation as an uncommonly skilled buffalo hunter and one of the army's most daring western scouts. Adding yet further to his celebrity was Cody's tendency to exaggerate his derring-do, and the glorification of some of his adventures in the "Buffalo Bill" dime novels.

In 1883 Cody turned to exploiting the romantic allure of his name, and of the western frontier in general, by touring with his Wild West Show. An extravaganza that combined sharpshooting and riding exhibitions with reenactments of colorful moments in the West's history, the show had enormous popular appeal. For many years it played to packed audiences in both America and Europe.

BUFFALO BILL

HON. W™ F. CODY.

DRAWN AND PRINTED EXPRESSLY FOR THE FOLIO, THE GREAT ILLUSTRATED MUSICAL JOURNAL OF AMERICA

Lithograph of William F. "Buffalo Bill" Cody, by Samuel Frizzell (1843–1895), between 1873 and 1890, published by J. H. Bufford's Sons. NPG

Harrison Ford (b. 1942) wore this fedora and leather jacket costume in *Raiders of the Lost Ark* and *Indiana Jones and the Last Crusade,* the 1980s adventure films about an archaeologist who goes on quests for lost treasures. Scholar-adventurer Indiana Jones's resourceful and ironic heroism endeared him to moviegoers. The three Indiana Jones films sparked a demand for the kind of clothing the hero wore, and Americans have appropriated these symbols of adventure into their daily lives.

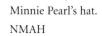

Minnie Pearl's hat.
NMAH

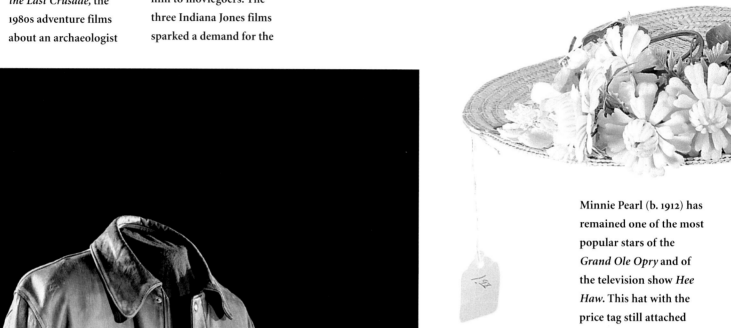

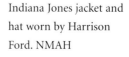

Indiana Jones jacket and hat worn by Harrison Ford. NMAH

Minnie Pearl (b. 1912) has remained one of the most popular stars of the *Grand Ole Opry* and of the television show *Hee Haw.* This hat with the price tag still attached symbolizes Minnie to all her fans. Her comic sketches of rural life in America were wonderful counterpoints to the often sad songs the country bands played. She has been beloved by generations of country music and humor fans.

Over the last thirty years—in large part due to the Grand Ole Opry and Minnie Pearl, among other country artists who appealed to a broad audience—country music has grown from a regional into a national and finally into an international phenomenon. Country music takes as its subject, the joys, sorrows, and tragedies of our everyday lives. This is the secret of its lasting appeal.

Star Trek, originally broadcast on NBC between 1966 and 1969, was a popular science fiction television series that inspired three other series and seven movies. Because a hallmark of science fiction is the representation of future technology, this phaser weapon was one of *Star Trek's* most significant props. The phaser is an incarnation of the classic ray gun from early science-fiction books and movies. It can stun, kill, or eradicate anything in its line of fire.

Star Trek has remained the most popular televised science fiction series to date. The original series' strong characters and plots often echoed the issues debated within American society and dealt with themes related to the Cold War. That underlying seriousness was at the heart of the show's appeal, and that appeal is still alive. "Trekkie" clubs have multiplied to the many thousands over the years, holding conventions, creating new characters, and reenacting famous scenes.

Star Trek phaser. NMAH

M*A*S*H signpost.
NMAH

M*A*S*H was a television series based on a movie and a book in which the actions that took place during one war reflected the issues of another. The award-winning comedy aired from 1972 to 1983 and continues in reruns. The show had a very loyal following, and some of its familiar props attained iconic status, including this signpost.

Although the series was set during the Korean War of the 1950s, most episodes commented on divisive events of the 1960s and 1970s—Watergate, feminism, and especially the Vietnam War. Episodes often stirred up controversies because of its ability to explore challenging, divisive, and often unpleasant issues. The hard work of the cast and crew of *M*A*S*H*, along with the thought that went into creating every episode, allowed the show to receive a total of 99 Emmy nominations and to win 14 Emmys. The final episode was the most-watched program of all time when it aired in 1983.

Paul Robeson (1898–1976) began his adult life as a lawyer. But because opportunities for African Americans in that profession were severely limited, he eventually gravitated to the stage. The vocational shift proved fortunate. When the largely self-trained Robeson appeared as the lead in Eugene O'Neill's *The Emperor Jones* in 1924, critics proclaimed him a natural actor. Other triumphs soon followed, not least of which was his 1930 performance as Shakespeare's Othello. The actor's rich baritone voice won him singing roles, and his rendition of "Ol' Man River" in *Show Boat* numbers among the unforgettable moments in the history of musicals.

Robeson's resentment over racial discrimination eventually led to his affiliation with several groups suspected of communist connections. As a result, amidst the fiercely anti-communist fervor that swept this country in the late 1940s, he was bitterly denounced, and his career as an actor for the most part ended.

Writer-photographer Carl Van Vechten encouraged Robeson to test him-

self as a singer shortly after his success in *The Emperor Jones*. Robeson made his debut as a concert singer in 1925, and he became as much admired for his singing as for his acting.

Photograph of Paul Robeson, by Carl Van Vechten, 1983 gelatin silver print from a 1933 negative. NPG

Ruby slippers, worn by Judy Garland in *The Wizard of Oz*. NMAH

Dorothy, played by Judy Garland (1922–69) in the 1939 MGM film *The Wizard of Oz*, wore these magical red slippers during her journey in a fantastic land and on her safe return home. Based on the 1900 novel by L. Frank Baum (1856–1919), the story had become a cartoon, a musical, and a silent picture before MGM created its hit movie, one of the first to use Technicolor film.

The slippers were central to the film's plot. Dorothy obtained them from the Good Witch and had to protect them from the Wicked Witch in order to return home. MGM personnel made several pairs of slippers for Garland to use during the filming—a common practice with important costumes and props. Garland wore this pair for dance scenes. The felt on the soles muffled her footsteps on the yellow brick road.

Kermit the Frog. NMAH

Kermit the Frog, created and activated by Jim Henson (1936–90), belongs to America's beloved puppet troop, the Muppets. Although he debuted on the Washington, D.C., television series *Sam and Friends* in 1957, Kermit has become best known as a star character on the public television show *Sesame Street*. Begun in 1969, the series revolutionized children's television by teaching lessons through colorful, boisterous, jazzy cartoons and live action scenes. Kermit acted as a master of ceremonies, comic, and crusader for tolerance. His hit song "It's Not Easy Being Green" treated the tensions caused by racial and ethnic difference in a playful way. Kermit moved with Henson to prime-time television and appeared in *The Muppet Show*. The series was so successful that it has inspired four Muppet movies.

American Sports

Most Americans love sports. As recreation, entertainment, and work for millions, sports provide significant shared experiences for this nation of immigrants. The players, spectators, and providers of sports—men and women from varied racial and ethnic backgrounds and economic circumstances—have all contributed to the American sporting experience. Across the country, at sports events or around radios and televisions, people have often found common ground in their passion for athletic contests. From these events, many gain strong individual, civic, ethnic, and national pride.

Sports reveal much about American society, highlighting the struggles and achievements of individuals and groups. Some athletes perform extraordinary physical feats, and others fight for a chance to play. All are winners, bringing the country closer to its ideals of equality and excellence. The Smithsonian's sports collections preserve objects representing sport on all levels—the ordinary and the extraordinary athlete, as well as sports fans and workers. The collections sustain our memories of our shared experiences of sport.

George Herman "Babe" Ruth (1895–1948) has been judged by many the greatest baseball player of all time. Also nicknamed the "Bambino" and the "Sultan of Swat," Ruth was a great fan favorite. His athletic excellence, high earnings, and flamboyant lifestyle appealed to the imaginations of the Americans who flocked to see him. Babe, in return, loved his fans and would autograph baseballs and other mementos for them.

Not merely famous, Babe Ruth was great. Born into extreme poverty, his talent was discovered at Baltimore's St. Mary's Industrial School for Boys. The Orioles—then a minor International League team with whom he first played in 1914—were unable to keep this brash kid who could both hit and pitch. After being sold by the Orioles to the Boston Red Sox, Ruth developed into the best left-handed pitcher in the American League. And he could hit. The Babe broke the major league home run record with 29 in 1918. After leading the Red Sox to two World Series titles, Ruth was traded to the New York Yankees, leading them to four titles. In his career, Babe hit 714 home runs, a record that stood until Hank Aaron broke it in 1974, almost forty years later.

After retiring in 1935, Ruth had hoped to manage a major league team, but his wild reputation prevented him from gaining a position of such responsibility. Lacking neither money nor adulation, he spent his last days making public appearances, doing his own radio show, playing golf, bowling, and fishing. A long-time smoker, he died at age 53 of throat cancer. At his funeral— an event on a par with President Franklin D. Roosevelt's—his teammate Waite Hoyt spoke for all Americans: "God, we liked that big s.o.b. He was a constant source of joy."

Baseball autographed by Babe Ruth. NMAH

Photograph of the Homestead Grays Baseball Team, by Charles "Teenie" Harris, 1993 gelatin silver print from a 1942 negative. NPG

Until Jackie Robinson broke baseball's color line to play with the Brooklyn Dodgers in 1947, the African American community expressed its passion for the country's "national pastime" by supporting separate baseball leagues. Among the most formidable teams were the Homestead Grays, a Pittsburgh-based team belonging to the Negro National League. The Grays dominated their league for many years and claimed nine championships between 1937 and 1946.

One of the reasons for the team's success was the catcher, Josh Gibson, standing third from left in the back row of this photograph. Often ranked among the greatest catchers in all of baseball, he was considered black baseball's answer to Babe Ruth. By the end of his career, his lifetime batting average stood at .350 and his home-run total at about 950. This photograph was the work of Charles "Teenie" Harris (b. 1908), who was for many years a chief photographer for the weekly African American newspaper, the *Pittsburgh Courier*.

Portrait of Joe Louis, by
Betsy Graves Reyneau,
1946, oil on canvas. NPG

Known to his fans as the
"Brown Bomber," boxer
Joe Louis (1914–81) lost
his first amateur bout in
two rounds in 1932. That
quick defeat may have
been humiliating to the
Detroit teenager, but it
was hardly a portent of
things to come. Between
1934, when he turned
professional, and 1949,
Louis lost only one
match. In 1937 he began a
twelve-year reign as box-
ing's world heavyweight
champion.

Regarded by many as
the best heavyweight of
all time, Louis had one of
his greatest moments on
June 22, 1938, when he
faced the boxer Max
Schmeling, one of Nazi
Germany's proudest sym-
bols of supposed Aryan
superiority. Louis
knocked Schmeling out
in a little over two min-
utes and won the admira-
tion of many Americans
who saw this triumph as
the ultimate debunking
of Hitler and his Nazi
racist theories.

This portrait was one
of a series of likenesses of
noted African Americans
done for the Harmon
Foundation, which
sought to heighten
awareness of black con-
tributions to this coun-
try's development.

Muhammad Ali (b. 1942) donated these gloves in 1976, shortly after his victorious fight to defend the heavyweight championship against Joe Frazier. Ali learned to box in order to keep bigger kids from stealing his bicycle. In 1960 he won the National Golden Gloves, the AAU title, and an Olympic gold medal, and he turned professional. Ali began his career as Cassius Clay but in 1964 changed his name to commemorate his conversion to the Nation of Islam. That year Ali won the heavyweight title for the first time, but he was stripped of it in 1968, after being convicted of refusing to obey the Vietnam draft. The Supreme Court overturned his conviction in 1970, and four years later Ali regained the world heavyweight title from George Foreman in the "Rumble in the Jungle" in Zaire. He was only the second man ever to recover the title. He successfully defended it against Frazier in 1975's "Thrilla in Manilla," considered the greatest fight in history.

After losing the title to Leon Spinks in February 1978, Ali managed to win it back from him for a third and final time later that year. His final contest took place in 1981. He retired and became a minister for the Nation of Islam. As he said, he was indeed "the Greatest."

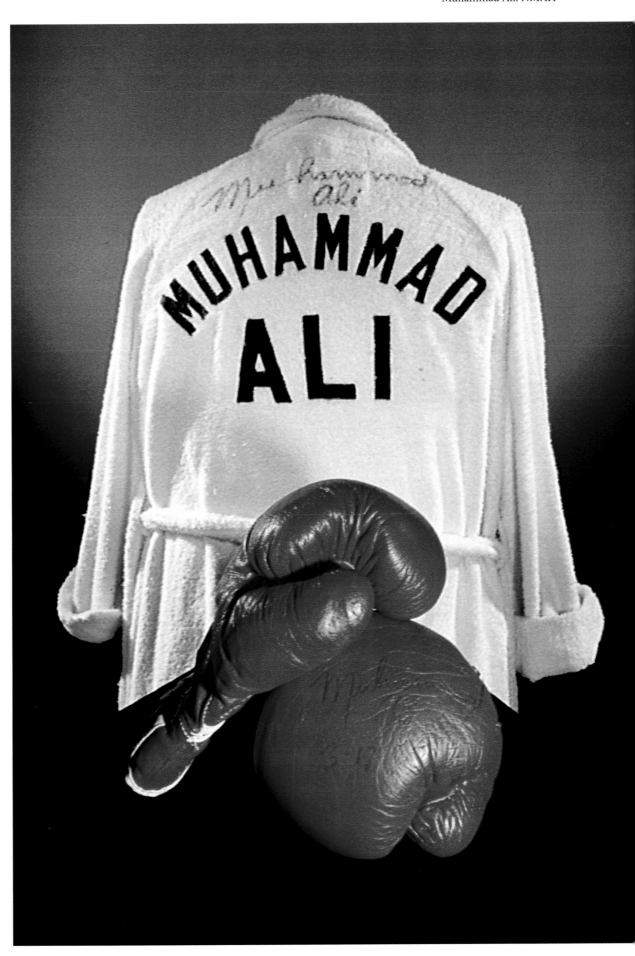

Tennis racket owned by
Chris Evert. NMAH

Chris Evert (b. 1954) was one of the top female tennis players in the 1970s and 1980s. Her silent and determined attitude—along with her steady baseline playing style—made her an extremely successful competitor. Evert won more than 100 titles, including the French Open, the U.S. Open, and Wimbledon. High points in her career often occurred when she competed with Martina Navratilova. A friendly and respectful, yet seriously competitive, relationship developed between the two women, creating one of the best rivalries in tennis.

Evert ultimately won more than $1 million playing tennis, and she won the Sports Woman of the Year Award in 1976. She was the first woman to accomplish either goal. Evert was inducted into the Interational Tennis Hall of Fame in 1995. Through all of her successes, her composure and ability to handle herself well made her fans think of her as the all-American girl. Evert became a role model for thousands of young women throughout America and the world.

Tennis racket owned by
Arthur Ashe. NMAH

Arthur Ashe (1943–93) bought this tennis racket in 1975 and used it in competitions from Wimbledon to the Davis Cup. He had begun his tennis career in Virginia in 1955. He competed successfully while a student at UCLA and as a U.S. Army officer. Early on he found racial prejudice one of his toughest challenges, preventing him and other African Americans from competing in prestigious tournaments. Like Althea Gibson before him, he successfully broke racial barriers to become a Grand Slam tournament winner and eventually the Davis Cup team cap-

tain. Ashe led groups, including the Black Tennis and Sports Association, that fostered the development of black athletes. His intense social concerns led him to write a three-volume work entitled *A Hard Road to Glory* on the athletic achievements of African Americans.

Like his life, his death served to help others. His early demise from complications caused by the AIDS virus—contracted through a blood transfusion—showed the country and the world that the disease presents an extremely serious threat to the entire human race.

NASCAR stock car, 1984,
driven by Richard Petty.
NMAH

Curb Motorsports con-
structed this Pontiac to
compete in the 1984
series of Grand National
races sanctioned by the
National Association for
Stock Car Auto Racing.
On July 4, 1984, Richard
Petty (b. 1937) drove the
car, bearing his traditional number 43, to first
place in the Firecracker
400 race at Daytona

Beach, Florida. This fin-
ish gave Petty his 200th
Grand National victory,
an unmatched achieve-
ment.

Capable of speeds of
more than 200 miles per
hour, this car was spe-
cially built for the "super
speedway" tracks at
Daytona and Talladega,
Alabama. The V-8 engine,
extensively modified

from a General Motors
block, produced 630
horsepower in dynamo-
meter tests. The roll cage,
harness and fire suppres-
sion equipment greatly
improved the driver's
safety. The car is set up
for the event in which it
last ran—the Talladega
500 on July 29, 1984.

Both an ice skater and a movie star, Sonja Henie (1912–69) significantly influenced the development of her sport with her blend of athletic skill and glamour. One of the great figure skaters of the 20th century, Norwegian-born Henie revived public interest in the sport with her three gold-medal performances at the Olympic Games, her touring ice pageants, and her spectacular movies.

Henie created a stir when she first competed in the 1924 Olympics at the age of eleven. In the 1920s and 1930s, she created the dance style of skating and the short skating costume, as well as popularized white boot skates for women—all innovations now part of the figure skater's traditional look. Through her ice shows and eleven movies, including *Sun Valley* (1941), Henie brought skating to a mass audience, attracting unprecedented media and spectator interest. Of skating, she mused "it's a feeling of ice miles running under your blades, the wind splitting open to let you through, the earth whirling around you at the touch of your toe, and speed lifting you off the ice far from all things that can hold you down."

Ice skates used by Sonja Henie. NMAH

Craig, Michael Eruzione, John Harrington, Steve Janaszak, Mark Johnson, Robert McClanahan, Kenneth Morrow, John O'Callahan, Mark Pavelich, Michael Ramsey, William Schneider, David Silk, Eric Strobel, Bob Suter, Philip Verchota, and Mark Wells became national heroes. People who had never watched hockey became dedicated fans. Beating the Soviets in the semifinal game became as important as, if not more important than, winning the gold medal itself.

U.S. Olympic Hockey Team Jersey, 1980. NMAH

At the 1980 Olympics in Lake Placid, New York, the United States' hockey team beat the favored Finnish team in the finals to win the gold medal. It was the semifinal game against the Soviet team, however, that created "the miracle on ice." A group of college athletes who had been playing together for only a few weeks achieved that feat when it beat the strong and experienced national team of the Soviet Union. The significance of the victory was heightened by the political climate of the time. In 1979 American embassy personnel had been taken hostage in Iran and held captive for over a year. The economy was in decline, and many Americans felt as if they were being held hostage by oil companies when gasoline prices soared.

The victory over the Soviet team gave a sorely needed boost to the American psyche. That day coach Herb Brooks and team members William Baker, Neal Broten, David Christian, Steve Christoff, James

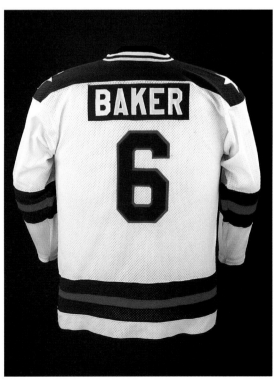

The Smithsonian Institution Museums

THE CASTLE

In 1847 work began on the Smithsonian's first building, the red sandstone "Castle" James Renwick designed. For more than thirty years after its completion in 1855, the Castle contained the Institution's laboratories, offices, art gallery, and natural history specimens. It also served as a home for Secretary Joseph Henry and his family and as a residence for bachelor scientists. In 1865 a fire destroyed the roof of the building's central section, together with most of the institution's early records. During the 1880s, much of the Castle was remodeled and enlarged. It now serves as the Smithsonian's administrative headquarters and houses the Smithsonian Information Center for visitors.

ARTS AND INDUSTRIES BUILDING

The Arts and Industries Building, adjacent to the Castle, was designed to meet the Institution's need for more exhibition space after it acquired material from the 1876 Centennial Exposition in Philadelphia. Originally known as the National Museum Building, it was first used on March 4, 1881, for President James Garfield's inaugural ball. The museum was renamed in 1910, when all the natural history collections (including fossils, minerals, and gems) were moved to the new Natural History Building. The remaining collections (including musical instruments, postage stamps, and first ladies gowns) were moved in 1964 to the newly opened Museum of History and Technology, leaving only an aeronautics exhibit in the Arts and Industries Building. Today, the building is the site of "1876: A Centennial Exhibition," which was installed for the U.S. bicentennial celebrations in 1976.

THE NATIONAL ZOOLOGICAL PARK

In 1888 and again in 1890, an Act of Congress provided for a National Park to be established under the Smithsonian's aegis on a 175-acre tract in Washington's Rock Creek Park. The National Zoo's collections began with a small menagerie—

including a few buffalo—maintained behind the Castle. Today the Zoo's innovative biopark approach gives visitors a perspective on the natural world based on the awareness of the countless processes that link all life on earth and the earth itself.

NATIONAL MUSEUM OF AMERICAN ART

In 1903 Harriet Lane Johnson, the niece of President James Buchanan, died and left her art collection to the Smithsonian. Today her bequest is part of the National Museum of American Art, home to the largest collection of American art in the world. The museum holds some 35,000 works reflecting the nation's ethnic, geographic, and religious diversity. It has previously been known as the National Gallery of Art and the National Collection of Fine Arts.

NATIONAL MUSEUM OF NATURAL HISTORY

The third Smithsonian building erected on the National Mall was the granite-faced Natural History Building, at one time called the new National Museum. Although construction was not completed until 1911, its staff began to move collections into the building in 1909. In 1969 its official name became the National Museum of Natural History. The National Museum of Natural History is devoted to research, collection, and exhibition in the fields of biology, earth sciences, and anthropology.

FREER GALLERY OF ART

Upon his death in 1904, industrialist Charles Lang Freer willed his art collection to the nation. In 1923 the Freer Gallery of Art opened to the public. The gallery features Asian art, as well as the largest group of works by James McNeill Whistler in the United States.

NATIONAL MUSEUM OF AMERICAN HISTORY

In 1955 Congress authorized construction of a building for the National Museum of History and Technology. The museum opened in 1964. It was an immediate success, and by the end of the year, it had been visited by 5.4 million people. In 1980 it was renamed the National Museum of American History. Its mission is to honor the heritage of the American people by collecting, preserving, researching, and exhibiting their artifacts.

NATIONAL PORTRAIT GALLERY

The permanent collection of the National Portrait Gallery contains more than 11,000 paintings posters, photographs, prints, sculptures, and drawings of men and women who have made significant contributions to the history, development, and culture of the people of the United Sates. The gallery, which opened to the public in 1968, shares its home with the National Museum of American Art in the historic Old Patent Office Building.

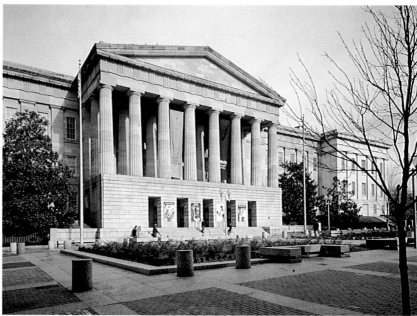

RENWICK GALLERY

The Renwick Gallery, a branch of the National Museum of American Art, is located across the street from the White

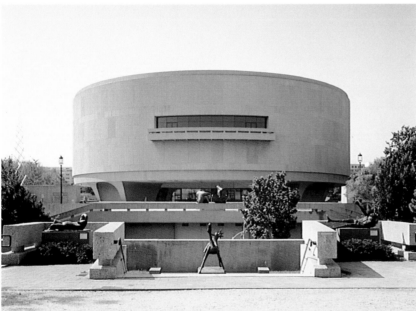

House. It serves as a showcase for American crafts, design, and decorative arts. It opened in 1972 in a building designed by James Renwick, the architect of the Smithsonian Castle.

ANACOSTIA MUSEUM

The Anacostia Museum, which opened as the Anacostia Neighborhood Museum in 1967, is devoted to interpreting the African American experience. Originally intended to function as a community-based neighborhood museum, the Anacostia Museum has evolved into a national resource for information on African American history and culture. It is located in Fort Stanton Park in southeast Washington.

THE HIRSHHORN MUSEUM AND SCULPTURE GARDEN

The Hirshhorn Museum and Sculpture Garden, devoted to contemporary and modern art, was created by an Act of Congress in 1966 to house the collection donated to the Smithsonian by Joseph H. Hirshhorn. The collection consists of 19th- and 20th-century sculpture, paintings, prints, and drawings. The museum and sculpture garden opened to the public in 1974.

COOPER-HEWITT, NATIONAL DESIGN MUSEUM

The Cooper-Hewitt, National Design Museum is the only museum in the United States devoted exclusively to the study and exhibition of historical and contemporary design. Located in the historic Andrew Carnegie mansion in New York City, the museum opened to the public in 1976.

NATIONAL AIR AND SPACE MUSEUM

The National Air Museum was established by law in August 1946. Twenty years later, the mission of the museum was amended to include the development of space flight and the name was changed to the National Air and Space Museum. During the museum's early years, exhibitions and other public activities were housed in the Arts and Industries Building and in temporary structures behind the Castle. Air and Space—the world's most visited museum—opened to the public on July 4, 1976.

NATIONAL MUSEUM OF AFRICAN ART

The National Museum of African Art is dedicated to collecting, studying, and displaying traditional arts from sub-Saharan Africa. Founded as a private educational institution in 1964, the museum became part of the Smithsonian in 1979. In 1987 the Museum of African Art moved from Capitol Hill to the National Mall, occupying part of the Quadrangle Complex, a largely underground facility .

ARTHUR M. SACKLER GALLERY

The Arthur M. Sackler Gallery opened in 1987 and shares part of the Quadrangle Complex underground facility with the Museum of African Art. The Sackler Gallery's permanent collection contains nearly 1,000 masterpieces of Asian art donated by Dr. Arthur M. Sackler (1913–87), a New York City art collector, philanthropist, research physician, and medical publisher.

NATIONAL POSTAL MUSEUM

The National Postal Museum opened in 1993 in the restored Washington City Post Office Building. The museum houses artifacts documenting the history of the nation's postal service and a philatelic collection—the largest of its kind in the world—with more than 16 million objects.

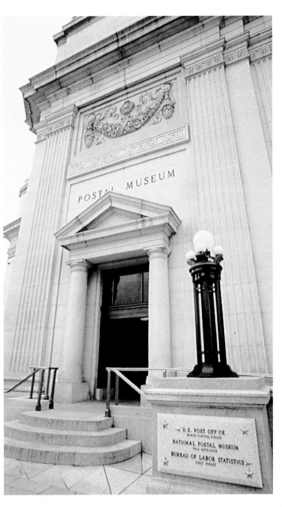

NATIONAL MUSEUM OF THE AMERICAN INDIAN'S GEORGE GUSTAV HEYE CENTER

The George Gustav Heye Center, part of the National Museum of the American Indian, is located in the historic Alexander Hamilton U.S. Customs House in New York City. Opened in 1994, this new facility will join the National Museum of the American Indian, still to be built on the National Mall in Washington, as the focus of the Smithsonian's Native American collections.

Staff and Acknowledgments

The staff of the *America's Smithsonian* exhibition

J. Michael Carrigan, Project Director
Ellen J. Dorn, Project Manager
Deena Gift, Logistics Manager
Meg Little, Logistics Manager
Marilyn Marton, Counselor to the Under Secretary
Fritz Baetz, Fund Manager
Todd Fuller, Ticketing Coordinator
Jennifer Bride, Gallery Manager
Kirsten Murray, Gallery Manager
Robert Heaton, Gallery Manager
Adrian Ahern, Assistant Gallery Manager
Bill Yardley, Media Liaison
Carol Harsh, Scheduling Coordinator
Helen Snyder, Volunteer Coordinator
Ikuko Shobayashi, Administrative Assistant
Carol H. Odom, Administrative Assistant
Jill Chappell, Administrative Assistant
Melinda Hale Lamont-Havers, Administrative Assistant

Jeffrey L. Brodie, Curatorial Coordinator
Tracy Goldsmith, Curatorial Project Specialist
Chris Shaffer, Curatorial Project Specialist
Kerry Hamilton, Graphics Coordinator
Marcia Daft, Education Outreach Coordinator
Diana Brinckman, Educational Outreach Coordinator
David Wallick, Educational Outreach Assistant
Joan Mathys, Video Researcher
Kay Fleming, Editor

Nigel Briggs, Design Manager
Erin Galbraith, Exhibit Designer
Walter Gomez, Exhibit Designer
Alex Rasputko, Exhibit Designer
Kathleen Tobin, Exhibit Designer
Brendan Traceski, Exhibit Designer
Stefanie Zarin, Design Assistant
Michael Donovan, Contract Administrator

Tracey Shields, Conservation Coordinator
Jeffrey Kimball, Objects Conservator
Martha Simpson, Objects Conservator
Rebecca Engelhardt, Bracket Coordinator

Rachel-Ray Cleveland, Paper Conservator
Elizabeth Wendelin, Paper Conservator
Virginia Lee Pledger, Textile Conservator
Stephen Collins, Textile Conservator
Samantha Alderson, Ethnographic Conservator
Lisa Kronthal, Ethnographic Conservator
Barbara Allen, Installation Conservator
Steve Weintraub, HVAC Consultant
James Hascall, Seismic Bracket Consultant
David Diggs La Touche, Bracket Maker
Charlie Bessant, Bracket Maker
Robert Fugelstad, Bracket Maker
Brian Jensen, Bracket Maker

John Fulton, Collections Management Coordinator
Merrill Lavine, Registrar
Wendy Turman, Registrar
Tom Yarker, Registrar
Ruth Ann Uithol, Traveling Registrar
Andrew Wallace, Traveling Registrar

Amy Featherston, Administrative Intern
Karyl Lin, Administrative Intern
Keith Haran, Curatorial Intern
James Nelson, Graphic Intern
Jennifer Faigin, Design Intern
Matthew Grandstaff, Design Intern
Amy Jones, Design Intern

The *America's Smithsonian* exhibition appreciates the volunteer efforts of the following individuals for reading and commenting upon the exhibition script: Brian R. Sullivan, Elizabeth Olendzki de Mijolla, Sister Mary Robertine Severens

All photographs by the Office of Printing and Photographic Services
James H. Wallace, Jr., Director
Mark Avino, Ralph Bagget, Eric Baum, Ricardo Blanc, Chip Clark, Jeff Crespi, Pamela Dewey, Harold Dorwin, Michael Fischer, Katherine Fogden, Karen Furth, Larry Gates, Carmelo Guadagno, Carl Hansen, Robb Harrel, Jim Hayden, David Heald, Janine Jones, Franko Khoury, Vic Krantz, Eric F. Long,

Diane L. Nordeck, Bruce Miller, Laurie Minor-Penland, John Parnell, Dane A. Penland, Jeff Ploskonka, Lee Stalsworth, Richard W. Strauss, Jeff Tinsley, John Tsantes, Ricardo Vargas, John White, Gene Young
Special thanks to: Lorie Aceto, David Burgevin, John Dillaber, Doc Dougherty, Donna Green, Nicholas J. Parrella, Teri Spruell

The staff of the *America's Smithsonian* exhibition appreciates the widespread cooperation and support of the many museums, libraries, archives, and research facilities of the Smithsonian Institution. We gratefully acknowledge the assistance of curators, specialists, and editors who contributed their expertise and knowledge to the exhibition. Special thanks to the conservators, registrars, and collection managers for the monumental task of preparing the objects for the traveling exhibition. The creation of the *America's Smithsonian* exhibition required the talents and support of countless Smithsonian staff members beyond those names listed here. We thank everyone who has participated in this tremendous effort.

NATIONAL AIR AND SPACE MUSEUM
Robert Hoffmann, Acting Director
Amanda Young, Liaison
Dorothy Cochrane, Karl Heinzel, Peter Jakab, Howard Kirschner, Richard Leyes, Allan Needell, Bill Reese, Bob Van Der Linden, Lillie Wiggins

NATIONAL MUSEUM OF AFRICAN ART
Sylvia Williams, Director
Steve Mellor, Liaison
Joan Amick, Keith Conway, Bryna Freyer, Christraud Geary, Julie Haifley, Madeleine Hexter, Janice Kaplan, Franko Khoury, Dana Moffett, Andrea Nicolls, Lydia Puccinelli, Philip Ravenhill, Jeffrey Smith, Amy Staples, Roslyn Walker

NATIONAL MUSEUM OF AMERICAN ART
Elizabeth Broun, Director
Melissa Kroning, Liaison

Courtney DeAngelis, David DeAnna, Hunter Hollins, Helen Ingalls, Martin Kotler, Virginia Mecklenburg, Stefano Scafetta, Jacquelyn Serwer, Michael Smallwood, Abigail Torrones, Katie Ziglar

ARCHIVES OF AMERICAN ART
Liza Kirwin, Liaison
Beth Joffrion, Susan Marcotte, Cindy Ott, Judy Throm

RENWICK GALLERY
Ellen M. Myette, Liaison
Jeremy Adamson

NATIONAL MUSEUM OF AMERICAN HISTORY
Spencer Crew, Director
Kate Henderson, Liaison
Spencer Crew would like to acknowledge the entire staff of the National Museum of American History and thank them for their dedicated support to the *America's Smithsonian* exhibition.

NATIONAL MUSEUM OF THE AMERICAN INDIAN
Richard West, Director
Clara Sue Kidwell and Mary Jane Lenz, Liaisons
Eulalie Bonar, Lee Callander, George Horse Capture, Kevin DeVorsey, Ann Drumheller, Susan Heald, Marian Kaminitz, Ramiro Matos, Scott Merritt, Nancy Rosoff, Tim Ramsey, Ken Yazzie

ANACOSTIA MUSEUM
Steven Newsome, Director
Sharon Reinckins, Liaison

HIRSHHORN MUSEUM AND SCULPTURE GARDEN
James Demetrion, Director
Judith Zilczer, Liaison
Lee Aks, Neal Benezr, Valerie Fletcher, Laurence Hoffman, Brian Kavanaugh, Anne-Louise Marquis, Dan Murray, Douglas J. Robinson, Phyllis Rosenzweig, Edward Schiesser, Lee Stalsworth, Ann Stetser

NATIONAL MUSEUM OF NATURAL HISTORY
Donald Ortner, Acting Director
Sally Love and Mary Jo Arnoldi, Liaisons
JoAllyn Archambault, Frederick

Bayer, Anna K. Behrensmeyer, Michael Brett-Surman, Carol Butler, Steven Cairns, Jennifer Clark, Susan Crawford, Diane Cloyd, Jonathan Coddington, Tim Coffer, Margaret Collins, William DiMichele, Carla Dove, Robert Emry, Douglas Erwin, Nathan Erwin, Natalie Firnhaber, Russell Feather, William Fitzhugh, Mark Florence, Raye Germon, Frederick Grady, Greta Hansen, Gary Hevel, Chang-su Houchins, Deborah Hull-Walski, Francis Hueber, Johanna Humphrey, Steven Jabo, Pegi Jodry, Adrienne Kaeppler, Brian Kensley, James Krakker, Peter Kroehler, Derrick Kysar, Conrad Labandeira, Robert Laughlin, Roxy Laybourne, Stephen Loring, Glen MacPherson, Patricia Nutter, David Pawson, Felicia Pickering, Jeffrey Post, Rick Potts, Paul Powhat, Robert Purdy, Raymond Rye, Robert Robbins, Carolyn Rose, Carol Sadler, Linda Schramm, Dennis Stanford, Warren Steiner, William Sturtevant, Robert Sullivan, Don Tenoso, Jean Thompson, Gus Van Beek, Jane Walsh, Scott Wing

NATIONAL PORTRAIT GALLERY
Alan M. Fern, Director
Suzanne Jenkins, Liaison
Joanna Britto, Carolyn K. Carr, Beverly Jones Cox, Barbara A. Hart, Ellen Miles, Cindy Lou Ockershausen, Mary Panzer, Wendy Reaves, Ann Shumard.

NATIONAL POSTAL MUSEUM
James H. Bruns, Director
Ted Wilson, Liaison
Kevin Allen, Linda Edquist, Joseph Geraci, Sanghmitra Kundu, Mary Lawson, Nancy Pope, Patricia Raynor, Elizabeth Wendelin

COOPER-HEWITT, NATIONAL DESIGN MUSEUM
Dianne H. Pilgrim, Director
Cordelia Rose, Liaison
Konstanze Bachmann, Lucy Commoner, Gail S. Davidson, Barbara Duggan, John Fell, Gregory Herringshaw, Eliza-

beth Horowitz, Katherine Keller, Steven Langehough, David R. McFadden, Gillian Moss, Brad Nugent, Brent Rummage, Paul Serrano, Deborah S. Shinn, Larry Silver, Milton Sonday, Marilyn Symmes, Cynthia Plaut Trope, Joanne Warner, Matthew Weaver

ARTHUR M. SACKLER GALLERY
Milo C. Beach, Director
Bruce Young, Liaison
Louise Cort, Vidya Dehijia, Massumeh Farhad, Ann Gunter, Tony Lake, Thomas W. Lentz, Jane Norman, Jenny So, Jan Smart, John Tsantes, Ann Yonemura

OFFICE OF SMITHSONIAN INSTITUTION ARCHIVES
Pamela M. Henson, Historian and Liaison
Alan L. Bain, William E. Cox, Terrica M. Gibson, Susan E. Glenn, Ethel Hedlin, Bruce Kirby, Frank R. Millikan, Tammy Peters, Marc Rothenberg, James A. Steed, Paul Theerman, Lynn M. Wojcik, Ashley Wyant

SMITHSONIAN INSTITUTION LIBRARIES
Barbara J. Smith, Director
Nancy Matthews, Liaison
Bill Baxter, Nancy E. Gwinn, Diane Shaw, Janice Stagnitto, Leslie Overstreet

OFFICE OF ARCHITECTURE AND HISTORIC PRESERVATION
Richard Stamm, Keeper, Castle Collection
Michael Hendron, Peter Muldoon

SMITHSONIAN ASTROPHYSICAL OBSERVATORY
Irwin I. Shapiro, Director
James C. Cornell, Jr.

SMITHSONIAN TROPICAL RESEARCH INSTITUTE
Ira Rubinoff, Director
Lucy Dorick, Lisa Barnet

SMITHSONIAN ENVIRONMENTAL RESEARCH CENTER
David L. Correll, Director
A. Mark Haddon

NATIONAL ZOOLOGICAL PARK
Michael H. Robinson, Director
Marc. B. Bretzfelder, Susan E. Haser, Robert J. Hoage, Herman P. Krebs, Michael J. Morgan

CENTER FOR FOLKLIFE PROGRAMS AND CULTURAL STUDIES
Richard Kurin, Director
Jeff Place

150TH ANNIVERSARY COORDINATING COMMITTEE
Marc Pachter, Chair
Alice Burnette, John Berry, Ron Cuffe, Barbara Hart, Richard Kurin, Nancy Johnson, Rick Johnson, Melissa Levine, Anna Martin, Marie Mattson, Claire Muldoon, Steve Newsome, Mike Robinson, Clyde Roper, Pat Sears, Marsha Shaines, David Umansky, L. Carole Wharton

UNDER SECRETARY'S STRATEGIC PLANNING GROUP
Constance Berry Newman, Chair
Roland Banscher, Tom Bresson, J. Michael Carrigan, John Cobert, Anna Cohn, Ellen Dorn, Marilyn Marton, Marie Mattson, Steven Placek, Marsha Shaines, David Umansky

AMERICA'S SMITHSONIAN CURATORIAL COMMITTEE
Anna Cohn, Chair
Mary Jo Arnoldi, Miguel Bretos, Lonnie Bunch, Richard Kurin, Virginia Mecklenburg, David McFadden, Marc Pachter, Jenny So, Robert Sullivan, Rosalyn Walker, Judith Zilczer

Several other offices have been instrumental in the planning and success of the America's Smithsonian exhibition. We especially thank Steven Placek for his assistance in coordinating and supervising all aspects of the security contracts. Under the direction of Tom Bresson, the Office of Protection Services has ensured the safety of the Smithsonian collections while traveling throughout the United States. Special thanks to David Voyles, Bobby Collins,

James Deely, Samuel Dews, Peter Mackessy, and Michael Pickett for coordinating and conducting the escorts of the artifacts. Jacqueline Young, Pat Terry, and Katherine Tkac of the Office of Risk and Asset Management have provided further assistance in identifying and resolving potential risks to the objects. Marsha Shaines and Lauryn Grant of the Office of the General Counsel provided legal advice and guidance to the exhibition.

The Office of Membership and Development staff have provided their energy and skills to provide the financial support for the America's Smithsonian exhibition. We especially thank Marie Mattson, Director; Judie Boerger, Special Assistant; and Susan Bradley, Corporate Partner Program Project Manager. Special thanks also to Twenty-first Century Marketing, whose president is Robert Prazmark.

John W. Cobert, director and contracting officer of the Office of Contracting and Property Management, would like to acknowledge the entire office staff for their dedication and skill in providing contract planning, formation, implementation, and management for the exhibition. Special thanks to Paulette Pressley, Lynn Spurgeon, Ron Cuffe, Judy Petroski, John Howser, Carol Ailes, Bruce Aronson, Brian Biggs, Nancy Chicoski, Adrienne Hedman, Melissa Howard, Tandra Jones, Melissa Levine, Lloyd McGill, Merna Rivenbank, and Jennifer Smith.

Finally, special thanks to the Smithsonian Institution Office of Public Affairs for orchestrating the media relations for this special event. The assistance and support of David Umansky, Linda St. Thomas, Vicki Moeser, and Margaret Pulles is greatly appreciated.

Illustration Credits

P. xiii: portrait of young Smithson, Smithsonian Institution, 72-3961

P. xiv: intaglio engraving of James Smithson, courtesy of the Smithsonian Archives, Larry Gates, 95-4933; British gold sovereign, courtesy of the National Museum of American History, transfer from the U.S. Department of the Treasury, U.S. Mint, Richard W. Strauss, 95-3573

P. xv: Jackson's letter, Smithsonian Institution, 73-13509; portraits of Henry and Baird, Smithsonian Archives, SA-16, SA-243

P. xvi: Smithson medal, courtesy of the National Museum of American History, Richard W. Strauss, 95-3573; Smithsonian mace, courtesy of the Castle Collection, Office of Architectural History, Smithsonian Institution, Jeff Ploskonka, 83-12714

P. xvii: photographs of the Castle and Arts and Industries Building, Smithsonian Institution, 93-2053, 4996;

P. 5: fossil shark jaws, courtesy of the National Museum of Natural History, Chip Clark, 95-40677

Pp. 6-7: pterosaur, courtesy of the National Museum of Natural History, Laurie Minor-Penland, 95-9612

P. 7: allosaur foot, courtesy of the National Museum of Natural History, Laurie Minor-Penland, 95-9611

P. 9: trilobites, ammonite, and molars, courtesy of the National Museum of Natural History, Laurie Minor-Penland, 95-9615

P. 10: fossil ammonites and belemnites, courtesy of the National Museum of Natural History, Chip Clark, 80-8409

P. 11: fossil crinoids, courtesy of the National Museum of Natural History, Laurie Minor-Penland, 95-9614

P. 12: duck-billed dinosaur skull, courtesy of the National Museum of Natural History, Laurie Minor-Penland, 95-9609

P. 13: diplodocus skull, courtesy of the National Museum of Natural History, Laurie Minor-Penland, 95-9613

P. 13: archaeopteryx, courtesy of the National Museum of Natural History, Vic Krantz, 85-681

P. 14: spider in amber, courtesy of the National Museum of Natural History, Laurie Minor-Penland, 95-9634

P 15: amber specimens (feather, termite, leaf), all courtesy of the National Museum of Natural History, Laurie Minor-Penland, 95-9635, 95-9632, 95-9636

P. 17: emerald specimens (Columbia and North Carolina), both courtesy of the National Museum of Natural History, Laurie Minor-Penland, 95-9627, 95-9620

P. 18: red beryl, aquamarine, and azurite, all courtesy of the National Museum of Natural History, Laurie Minor-Penland, 95-9628, 95-9629, 95-9630

P. 19: barite and dioptase, both courtesy of the National Museum of Natural History, Laurie Minor-Penland, 95-9626, 95-9568

P. 20: malachite, tourmaline, and opal, all courtesy of the National Museum of Natural History, Laurie Minor-Penland, 95-9622, 95-9624, 95-9537

P. 21: septarian nodule, courtesy of the National Museum of Natural History, Dane Penland, 95-9571

P. 22: wulfenite crystal, courtesy of the National Museum of Natural History, Chip Clark, 92-6522

P. 23: first day cover, courtesy of the National Museum of Natural History; copper, courtesy of the National Museum of Natural History, Chip Clark, 92-6532

P. 24: azurite, courtesy of the National Museum of Natural History, Chip Clark

P. 25: variscite crystal, courtesy of the National Museum of Natural History, Laurie Minor-Penland, 95-9607

P. 26: smithsonite specimens, all courtesy of the National Museum of Natural History, Laurie Minor-Penland, 95-9616

P. 27: fluorescents, all courtesy of the National Museum of Natural History, Carl Hansen, 95-9576, 95-9574

P. 28: spodumene crystal, courtesy of the National Museum of Natural History, Laurie Minor-Penland, 95-9623

P. 29: faceted topaz and spodumene and topaz crystal, all courtesy of the National Museum of Natural History, Laurie Minor Penland, 95-9617, 95-9625

P. 30: jadeite cobble, courtesy of the National Museum of Natural His- tory,, Laurie Minor-Penland, 95-9621

P. 31: jadeite carving, courtesy of the National Museum of Natural History, Dane Penland, 95-9569

P. 32: Nakhla and Canyon Diablo meteorites, both courtesy of the National Museum of Natural History, Laurie Minor-Penland, 95-9610, 95-9570

P. 33: Cuban land snails, General Mollusk Collection; imperial delphinus, General Mollusk Collection, donated by Roberta Cranmer. Both courtesy of the National Museum of Natural History, Carl Hansen, 95-9599, 95-9603

P. 34: murex, cockles, and cowries, all General Mollusk Collection, donated by Roberta Cranmer, courtesy of the National Museum of Natural History, Carl Hansen, 95-9603, 95-9597

P. 35: trumpet triton, geography cone, and marble cone, all General Mollusk Collection, donated by Roberta Cranmer, courtesy of the National Museum of Natural History, Carl Hansen, 95-9597, 95-9598, 95-9578

P. 36: Yoka star turban and staircase abalone, both General Mollusk Collection, donated by Roberta Cranmer, courtesy of the National Museum of Natural History, Carl Hansen, 95-9596

P. 37: scallops, mossy mopalia, and regal thorny oyster, all General Mollusk Collection, donated by Roberta Cranmer, courtesy of the National Museum of Natural History, Carl Hansen, 95-9594, 95-9600

P. 38: elephant tusk, donated by Roberta Cranmer; Formosan tusk and false Scorpio conch, donated by William Bledsoe. All General Mollusk Collection, courtesy of the National Museum of Natural History, Carl Hansen, 95-9600, 95-9596

P. 39: sun starfish, sea urchin, and reef coral, all courtesy of the National Museum of Natural History, Carl Hansen, 95-9592, 95-9595, 95-9591

P. 40: sea fans and deep-water coral, all courtesy of the National Museum of Natural History, Carl Hansen, 95-9591, 95-9593

P. 41: basket starfish, courtesy of the National Museum of Natural History, Carl Hansen, 95-9592

P. 42: Audubon painting, courtesy of the National Portrait Gallery, transfer from the National Gallery of Art, gift of the Avalon Foundation through the generosity of Ailsa Mellon Bruce, 1951, NPG.65.67

P 43: Audubon, *The Birds of America*, and Audubon and Bachman, *The Quadrupeds of North America*, both courtesy of the Smithsonian Institution Libraries, Richard W. Strauss, 95-5511-8, 95-5512-11

Pp. 44-45: beetles and weevils, all courtesy of the National Museum of Natural History, Carl Hansen, 95-9588, 95-9579, 95-9587, 95-9572, 95-9573, 95-9584

Pp. 46-47: butterfies and moths, all courtesy of the National Museum of Natural History, Carl Hansen, 95-9577, 95-9586, 95-9578, 95-9588, 95-9582, 95-9585

P. 48: Lewis & Clark compass and case, courtesy of the National Museum of Natural History, Ricardo Vargas, 95-2348

P. 49: Burgess Shale specimen, courtesy of the National Museum of Natural History, Doug Erwin

P. 50: drawing from Wilkes Expedition, courtesy of the Smithsonian Archives, Larry Gates, 95-4918; Wilkes, *Narrative of the United States Exploring Expedition ... 1849*, courtesy of the Smithsonian Institution Libraries, Richard W. Strauss, 95-5512-7

P. 51: Fiji club, Carl Hansen, 95-9602; and throwing club, Diane Nordeck, 84-10839-10/5A. Both courtesy of the National Museum of Natural History

P. 52: Orteig check, courtesy of the National Air and Space Museum, Mark Avino, 95-2379

P. 53: Earhart flight suit, courtesy of the National Postal Museum, Ricardo Vargas, 94-216

P. 54: Earhart cover, courtesy of the National Postal Museum, Larry Gates, 95-4936; Yeager jacket, courtesy of the National Air and Space Museum, Mark Avino, 95-2378

P. 55: Vin Fiz engine, gift of Ruth Jacobs, wife of Jim Jacobs, 1948, Mark Avino, 95-8263; Vin Fiz aircraft, Dane Penland, 80-2081. Both courtesy of the National Air and Space Museum

P. 56: Vanguard satellite, courtesy of the National Air and Space Museum, Mark Avino, 95-8269

P. 57: Surveyor vernier rocket engine, gift of the Jet Propulsion Lab, courtesy of the National Air and Space Museum, Mark Avino, 95-8262

P. 58: *Freedom 7* and Apollo 11 lunar maps, courtesy of the National Air and Space Museum, Mark Avino, 95-1557-8, 95-8264

P. 59: Apollo 14 command module, courtesy of the National Air and Space Museum, 94-251

P. 60: lunar rover, courtesy of the National Air and Space Museum, Mark Avino, 95-8265

P. 61: Apollo 15 space suit, courtesy of the National Air and Space Museum, Mark Avino, 95-2380

P. 64: Moore, *Draped Reclining Figure,* 1952-53, courtesy of the Hirshhorn Museum and Sculpture Garden, gift of Joseph H. Hirshhorn, 1966, Lee Stalsworth, 66.3634

P. 65: Hassam, *The South Ledges, Appledore,* courtesy of the National Museum of American Art, gift of John Gellatly, Michael Fischer, 1929.6.62

P. 66: Moran, *Mist in Kanab Canyon,* courtesy of the National Museum of American Art, gift of John Gellatly, Michael Fischer, 1942.11.10

P. 67: Church, *Aurora Borealis,* courtesy of the National Museum of American Art, gift of Eleanor Blodgett, Gene Young, 1911.4.1

P. 68: Catlin, *Corn, A Miniconjou Warrior,* courtesy of the National Museum of American Art, gift of Mrs. Joseph Harrison, Jr., Gene Young, 1985.66.78

P. 69: Eakins, *Mrs. Eakins,* courtesy of the Hirshhorn Museum and Sculpture Garden, gift of Joseph H. Hirshhorn, 1972, Lee Stalsworth, 66.1522

P. 70: Cassatt, *The Caress,* courtesy of the National Museum of American Art, gift of William T. Evans, Gene Young, 1911.2.1

P. 71: Sargent, *Mrs. Kate Moore,* 1884, courtesy of the Hirshhorn Museum and Sculpture Garden, gift of Joseph H. Hirshhorn, 1972, Lee Stalsworth 72.257

P. 72: Dewing, *Garden in May,* courtesy of the National Museum of American Art, gift of John Gellatly, Michael Fischer, 1929.6.26

P. 73: Sloan, *Ferry Slip, Winter,* 1905-6, courtesy of the Hirshhorn Museum and Sculpture Garden, gift of Joseph H. Hirshhorn, 1966, Lee Stalsworth, 66.4607

P. 74: Hopper, *11A.M.,* courtesy of the Hirshhorn Museum and Sculpture Garden, Lee Stalsworth, 66.2504

P. 75: photograph of Hopper by George Platt Lynes, February 21, 1950, courtesy of the Archives of American Art

P. 76: O'Keeffe, *Soft Gray, Alcalde Hill,* 1929-30, courtesy of the Hirshhorn Museum and Sculpture Garden, gift of Joseph H. Hirshhorn, 1972, Lee Stalsworth, 72.216

P. 77: photograph of O'Keeffe by Alfred Stieglitz, 1920, courtesy of the Archives of American Art

P. 78: Pippin, *Holy Mountain III,* 1945, courtesy of the Hirshhorn Museum and Sculpture Garden, gift of Joseph H. Hirshhorn, 1966, Lee Stalsworth, 66.4069

P. 79: Rodin, *Walking Man,* 1900, courtesy of the Hirshhorn Museum and Sculpture Garden, gift of Joseph H. Hirshhorn, 1966, Lee Stalsworth, 66.4343

P. 80: ritual food vessel, courtesy of the Arthur M. Sackler Gallery, gift of Arthur M. Sackler, John Tsantes, S1987.286

P. 81: gold finial, Monteria Dept. of Bolivar, Colombia, courtesy of the National Museum of the American Indian, presented by Harmon W. Hendricks, 1920, Karen

Furth, 10/507; box for betel nut and spices, courtesy of the Arthur M. Sackler Gallery, gift of Rajinder K. and Narinder K. Keith in honor of their father, Sardar Gurdit Singh Keith, Jim Hayden, S1987.969

P. 82: goat, courtesy of the Arthur M. Sackler Gallery, gift of Arthur M. Sackler, John Tsantes, S1987.18

P. 83: water dropper and jade double vase, courtesy of the Arthur M. Sackler Gallery, gift of Arthur M. Sackler, John Tsantes, S1987.796, S1987.725

P. 84: ornamental disk, courtesy of the Arthur M. Sackler Gallery, gift of Arthur M. Sackler, John Tsantes, S1987.922; slit gong, courtesy of the National Museum of African Art, museum purchase, Franko Khoury, 92-012-001

P. 85: ceramic vessel by Nampeyo, courtesy of the National Museum of the American Indian, Katherine Fogden, 21/4629

Pp. 86-89: Egyptian manuscript page; *A Pair of Lovers; A Demon Descends upon a Horseman; Old Woman and Two Sages in a Garden.* All courtesy of the Arthur M. Sackler Gallery, Smithsonian Unrestricted Funds, Smithsonian Collections Acquisition Program, and Dr. Arthur M. Sackler, Jeff Crespi, S1986.108, S1986.278, S1986.252, S1986.216

P. 90: Yoruba staff, purchased with funds from the Smithsonian Collections Acquisitions Program; Benin plaque, gift of Joseph H. Hirshhorn to the Smithsonian Institution, 1979. Both courtesy of the National Museum of African Art, Franko Khoury, 88-001-001, 85-019-018

P. 91: cylindrical vessel and bell, courtesy of the Arthur M. Sackler Gallery, gifts of Arthur M. Sackler, John Tsantes, S1987.341a/b, S1987.286

Pp. 92-95: Japanese porcelain jar, vases, plate, and bowl, courtesy of the Arthur M. Sackler Gallery, gifts of the Japan Foundation, Robb Harrel, S1993.19, S1993.23, S1993.31, S1993.32, S1993.38

P. 96: Iranian ewer, courtesy of the Arthur M. Sackler Gallery, gift of Arthur M. Sackler, John Tsantes, S87.118

P. 97: Miller pitcher, museum purchase made possible by the James Renwick Alliance and the Smithsonian Collections Acquisition Program; Bacerra teapot, gift of the James Renwick Alliance and Museum Purchase through the Smithsonian Collections Acquisitions Program. Both National Museum of American Art, Bruce Miller, 1988.71, 1990.78

P. 98: Porcella, *Takoage,* Renwick National Museum of American Art, museum purchase through the Smithsonian Collections Acquisition Program, Bruce Miller, 1995.15

P. 99: Riley table, commissioned for the African-American Design Archive at National Design Museum, Eric Baum, 1993-9-1; table lamp, originally owned by

Andrew Carnegie, gift of Margaret Carnegie Miller, 1977-111-1. Both courtesy of Cooper-Hewitt, National Design Museum

P. 100: Wright side chair, Cooper-Hewitt National Design Museum, gift of Tetsuzo Inumaru, John White, 1968-137-1a

P. 101: Gehry lounge chair, courtesy of Cooper-Hewitt, National Design Museum, gift of William Wolfenden, John White, 1988-79-2; Ngombe chair, courtesy of the National Museum of African Art, museum purchase, Franko Khoury, 90-004-001

P. 102: Jacques mermaid chair, courtesy of the Anacostia Museum, Harold Dorwin, 95-008, 95-009

P. 103: *Pintades (Guinea Fowls),* courtesy of the National Museum of African Art, museum purchase, Franko Khoury, 92-015-004

P. 104: silver place setting, courtesy of Cooper-Hewitt, National Design Museum, The Decorative Arts Association Acquisitions Fund in honor of John L. Marion, John White, 1990-137-1/9

P. 105: Wright place setting, courtesy of Cooper-Hewitt, National Design Museum, gift of Roger A. Kennedy, John Parnell, 1979-77-17

P. 106: gold pendant, courtesy of the National Museum of African Art, bequest of Mrs. Robert Woods Bliss, Franko Khoury, 69-020-001

P. 107: jade pendant, courtesy of the National Museum of the American Indian, David Heald, 23/9595

P. 108: Merriweather Post tiara and brooches gift of Mrs. Marjorie Merriweather Post, Laurie Minor-Penland; Star of Bombay, Dane Penland, 84-17944. Both courtesy of the National Museum of Natural History

P. 109: Mackay necklace, courtesy of the National Museum of Natural History, bequest of Anna Case Mackay, 1984, Dane Penland, 84-8597

P. 110: Hooker diamonds, courtesy of the National Museum of Natural History, gift of Mrs. Janet Annenberg Hooker, Laurie Minor-Penland, 94-1258f

P. 111: Pardon necklace, National Museum of American Art, gift of the James Renwick Alliance and Museum Purchase through the Smithsonian Collections Acquisitions Program, Bruce Miller, 1991.136

P. 112: Mawdsley bracelet, courtesy of the Renwick Gallery of the National Museum of American Art, gift of the James Renwick Alliance in honor of Lloyd E. Herman, Director Emeritus, Renwick Gallery, Bruce Miller, 1983.52; Harper, *Amuletic Beads #3,* National Museum of American Art, gift of Dr. and Mrs. Matthew M. Cohen, Bruce Miller, 1986.55. © 1987 William Harper

P. 113: Wilkerson ringdant, gift of Leonard E. and Victoria Wilkinson, Laurie Minor-Penland, 95-9618

P. 114: Catlett, *Singing Head,* courtesy of the National Museum of American Art, Gene Young, 1989.52

P. 115: Picasso, *Head,* 1934, courtesy of the Hirshhorn Museum and Sculpture Garden, bequest of Joseph H. Hirshhorn, 1981, Lee Stalsworth, 86.3801

P. 116: Leger, *Still Life: King of Diamonds,* 1927, courtesy of the Hirshhorn Museum and Sculpture Garden, gift of Joseph H. Hirshhorn, 1966, Lee Stalsworth, 66.2989

P. 117: Davis, *Hot Beat,* courtesy of the National Museum of American Art, gift of the Woodward Foundation, Gene Young, 1976.108.33

P. 118: photograph of Kuniyoshi by Max Yavno, 1941, courtesy of the Archives of American Art, AAA reel 440:1423

P. 119: Kuniyoshi, *Look, It Flies,* 1946, courtesy of the Hirshhorn Museum and Sculpture Garden, gift of Joseph H. Hirshhorn, 1966, Lee Stalsworth, 66.2856

P. 120: Noguchi, *Endless Coupling,* 1957, courtesy of the Hirshhorn Museum and Sculpture Garden, gift of Joseph H. Hirshhorn, 1966, Ricardo Blanc Noguchi, 66.3866

P. 121: Botero, *The Hunter,* 1980, courtesy of the Hirshhorn Museum and Sculpture Garden, gift of Fernando Botero, 1980, Lee Stalsworth, 80.111

P. 122: Estes, *Diner,* 1971, courtesy of the Hirshhorn Museum and Sculpture Garden, museum purchase, 1977, Lee Stalsworth, 77.75

P. 123: Warhol, *Flowers,* courtesy of the Hirshhorn Museum and Sculpture Garden, bequest of Joseph H. Hirshhorn, 1981, Lee Stalsworth, 86.5673

P. 124: Diebenkorn, *Man and Woman in Large Room,* courtesy of the Hirshhorn Museum and Sculpture Garden, gift of Joseph H. Hirshhorn, 1972, Lee Stalsworth, 66.1371

P. 125: Brown, *John Henry,* courtesy of the National Museum of American Art, gift of Gerald L. Pearson, Gene Young. © 1979 Frederick Brown

Pp. 126-27: Tucker '48 sedan, courtesy of the National Museum of American History, transfer from the U.S. Marshals Service, Ross Chapple. From *The Smithsonian: 150 Years of Adventure, Discovering, and Wonder* by James Conaway, Smithsonian Books, © 1995 Smithsonian Institution. Used with permission.

P. 130: carved stone bowl, courtesy of the National Museum of the American Indian, collected by Marco A. Soto and presented by Harmon W. Hendricks, Carmelo Guadagno, 6/1262

P. 131: ritual dagger-axe *(ge),* courtesy of the Arthur M. Sackler Gallery, gift of Arthur M. Sackler, John Tsantes, S1987.717

P. 132: Clovis points, courtesy of the National Museum of Natural History, Carl Hansen, 95-9604

P. 133: Cycladic figure, courtesy of the National Museum of Natural History, Carl Hansen, 95-9602

P. 134: hand axe, courtesy of the National Museum of Natural History, Carl Hansen, 95-9604

P. 135: relief panel, Piedras Negras, Peten Dept., Guatemala, courtesy of the National Museum of the American Indian, presented by Dr. and Mrs. Arthur M. Sackler, David Heald, 24/457

P. 136: Egyptian stele, courtesy of the National Museum of Natural History, presented as a Bicentennial Gift to the American People by the Egyptian President Anwar Sadat, Carl Hansen, 95-9590

P. 137: Bridge-handled vessel, Nazca, Dept. of Ica, Peru, courtesy of the National Museum of the American Indian, purchased in 1950 David Heald 21/6914

P. 138: Washington's sword and scabbard, courtesy of the National Museum of American History, transfer from the Department of State, 1922, Ricardo Vargas, 90-10106

P. 139: "porthole" portraits of Martha and George Washington, courtesy of the National Portrait Gallery, gifts of an anonymous donor, NPG.75.3, NPG.75.4

P. 140: Lincoln hat, courtesy of the National Museum of American History, transfer from the War Department, January 25, 1902, Ricardo Vargas, 95-5528

P. 141: Lincoln silver service, courtesy of the National Museum of American History, gift of Lincoln Isham, great-grandson of Abraham and Mary Todd Lincoln, 1957, Ricardo Vargas, 95-5506

P. 142: FDR lap robe, courtesy of the National Museum of American History, gift of Mr. James M. Snyder, Mrs. Monte C. Vanness, and Mrs. Joan M. Parker, the children of Mr. Frederick Montford "Monte" Snyder, the President's chauffeur, 1970, Richard W. Strauss; FDR microphone, courtesy of the National Museum of American History, gift of the Columbia Broadcasting System, Inc. (CBS) and WTOP-Radio, 1964. Richard W. Strauss, 95-5513-5

P. 143: FDR design and stamp, courtesy of the National Postal Museum, Larry Gates, 95-4935

P. 144: Roosevelt sculpture, courtesy of the National Portrait Gallery, NPG.74.16

P. 145: Kennedy gown, courtesy of the National Museum of American History, gift of Jacqueline Kennedy, 1962, Eric F. Long, 90-2510

P. 146: Nixon gown, gift of Patricia Ryan Nixon, 1969, Eric F. Long, 90-2507; Eisenhower gown, gift of Mrs. Dwight D. Eisenhower, 1953, 72-2438. Both courtesy of the National Museum of American History

P. 147: McKee gown, courtesy of the National Museum of American History, gift of Benjamin Harrison McKee and Mary McKee Reisinger, 1945, Eric F. Long, 92-1464-3

P. 148: Garfield gown, courtesy of the National Museum of American History, gift of Mrs. G. Stanley-Brown and the Garfield children, 1921, Diane Nordeck, 91-10693

P. 149: Cleveland dress, courtesy of the National Museum of American History, gift of the heirs under the estates of Richard F. and Jessie B. Cleveland, 1979, Eric F. Long, 92-3649-9

P. 151: Lincoln photo, courtesy of the National Portrait Gallery and the Polaroid Corporation, NPG.81.M1

P. 152: Lincoln mask, courtesy of the National Museum of American History, presented to the U.S. government by thirty-three subscribers, including Bram Stoker, Augustus St. Gaudens, and the Boston Athenaeum, Eric F. Long, 93-12714

P. 153: Douglass photo by George K. Warren, courtesy of the National Portrait Gallery, gift of Emma N. and Sidney Kaplan, NPG.91.75

Pp. 154-55: Appomattox furniture: Lee chair, bequest of Mrs. Bridget O'Farrell; table, bequest of Mrs. Elizabeth B. Custer; Grant chair, bequest from the estate of General Wilmon W. Blackmar. All courtesy of the National Museum of American History, Richard W. Strauss, 95-5515-7

P. 156: Lee sculpture by Edward Valentine, courtesy of the National Portrait Gallery, NPG.78.35

P. 157: Balling, *Ulysses S. Grant and His 26 Generals,* courtesy of the National Portrait Gallery, transfer from the Library of Congress, NPG.76.8

P. 159: Griffiths family keepsakes, all courtesy of the Anacostia Community Museum, bequest of the D. and J. Griffiths Estate, Harold Dorwin, 95-011, 95-010, 95-013, 95-017, 95-007

P. 160: Beckley wagon, courtesy of the National Museum of American History, gift of Don H. Berkebile, Eric F. Long, 95-5527

P. 161: Crow child's dress, courtesy of the National Museum of the American Indian, Katherine Fogden, 11/7692; Chinese American woman's dress, courtesy of the Museum of American History, gift of James Edgar Mead and Mrs. Virginia Lee Mead, Eric F. Long, 95-5526

P. 162: fishtrap basket, courtesy of the National Museum of Natural History, Diane Nordick, 95-20071

P. 163: Sans Arc Sioux man's shirt, courtesy of the National Museum of the American Indian, Janine Jones, 1/3920; Asante double figure, courtesy of the National Museum of African Art, acquisition grant from the James Smithson Society and museum purchase, Franko Khoury, 87-004-001

P. 164: dog sled, courtesy of the National Postal Museum, Richard W. Strauss and Eric F. Long, 95-5516A-4

P. 165: trickster doll, courtesy of the National Museum of Natural History, Carl Hansen, 95-9575

P. 166: stamps, courtesy of the National Postal Museum, Larry Gates, 95-4930, 95-4934

P. 167: Bethune portrait by Reyneau, courtesy of the National Portrait Gallery, gift of the Harmon Foundation, NPG67.78

P. 168: Chavez jacket, courtesy of the National Museum of American History, gift of Helen Chavez, Cesar Chavez's wife, 1993; Martinez, farm worker's altar, courtesy of the National Museum of American Art, gift of the International Bank of Commerce in honor of Antonio R. Sanchez, Sr., Gene Young, 1992.95

P. 169: photograph of Du Bois by Carl Van Vechten, courtesy of the National Portrait Gallery, NPG.80.25. Photograph © Estate of Carl Van Vechten. Gravure and compilation © Eakins Press Foundation

P. 170: Catlin, *Keokuk on Horseback,* courtesy of the National Museum of American Art, gift of Mrs. Joseph Harrison, Jr., 1985.66.1a

P. 171: portrait of Lafayette by Jouett, courtesy of the National Portrait Gallery, gift of the John Hay Whitney Collection, NPG.82.150

P. 172: photographs of King Kamehameha III and King Kamehameha IV, courtesy of the National Portrait Gallery, gifts of the Bernice Pauahi Bishop Museum, NPG.80.313, NPG.80.314

P. 173: bust of Washington by Barthé, courtesy of the National Portrait Gallery, NPG.73.22

P. 174: Portrait of Kennedy by Gardner Cox, courtesy of the National Portrait Gallery, gift of Gardner Cox, NPG.69.54

P. 175: photograph of King by Benedict J. Fernandez, courtesy of the National Portrait Gallery, gift of Benedict J. Fernandez, NPG.80.173

P. 176: Mexican mask, courtesy of the National Museum of Natural History, Diane Nordeck, 95-20069

P. 177: raven mask, courtesy of the National Museum of Natural History, Carl Hansen, 95-9601

P. 178: Yaure mask, courtesy of the National Museum of African Art, museum purchase, Franko Khoury, 91-021-001

P. 179: reliquary guardian figure, courtesy of the National Museum of African Art, acquisition grant from the James Smithson Society and museum purchase, Franko Khoury, 88-004-001

P. 180: Ghost Dance dress, courtesy of the National Museum of the American Indian, Pamela Dewey, 2/8574

P. 181: totem pole, courtesy of the National Museum of Natural History, Carl Hansen, 95-9606

P. 182: Aragon, *La Buena Pastora,* courtesy of the National Museum of American History, from Mrs. William C. F. Robards, 1961, Richard W. Strauss, 95-5506-7; *Milagro de la virgen de Hormigüeros,* courtesy of the National Museum of American History, from Mrs. Otto Pike, 1968, Eric F. Long 94-118

P. 183: Cong, courtesy of the Arthur M. Sackler Gallery, gift of Arthur M. Sackler, Jim Hayden, S1987.887

P. 184: Pickering quilt, courtesy of the National Museum of American History, gift of Dr. Robert S. Bell in honor of the Frank Bell family: Frank and Bertha Wickersham Bell and their children; Raymond Bell, Mary Bell Stone, William Pickering Bell, Richard Craig Bell, Dorothy Jo Bell Foster, Frances Bell Brantingham, Margaret Bell Koster, John Burton Bell, and Dr. Robert S. Bell, 91-5765

P. 185: quilt, courtesy of the National Museum of American History, gift of Mr. Stewart Dickson, 1963, Jeff Tinsley 89-10434

P. 186: bear claw necklace, courtesy of the National Museum of the American Indian, Katherine Fogden, 14/1174A, 14/1174B

P. 187: Kaapor feathered crown, courtesy of the National Museum of the American Indian, Janine Jones, 23/3283

P. 188: Pawnee eagle feather war bonnet, courtesy of the National Museum of the American Indian, Janine Jones, 20/6142

P. 189: Comanche feather headdress, courtesy of the National Museum of the American Indian, Janine Jones, 3/7140

P. 190: Bell telephone, courtesy of the National Museum of American History, gift of American Telephone and Telegraph, 1923, Eric F. Long, 95-5520

P. 191: photograph of Carver by Clifton Johnson, courtesy of the National Portrait Gallery, NPG.92.156

P. 192: Edison light bulb, gift of the Department of Engineering, Princeton University, 1961, 91-6526; Jarvik-7 artificial heart, gift of the University Medical Center of the University of Arizona, 1987, Ricardo Vargas, 95-5504-3. Both courtesy of the National Museum of American History

P. 193: photograph of Einstein by Philippe Halsman, courtesy of the National Portrait Gallery, NPG.79.249. Permission Albert Einstein Archives, The Hebrew University of Jerusalem, Israel. Photo by Philippe Halsman © Halsman Estate

P. 194: Morse telegraph key, from the Western Union Telegraph Company, July 14, 1897; Morse telegraph patent model, from the U.S. Patent Office. Both courtesy of the National Museum of American History, Eric F. Long, 74-2491, 74-2494

P. 195: Rillieux patent model, courtesy of the Anacostia Community Museum, Harold Dorwin, 95-012

P. 196: Singer sewing machine patent model, gift of the Singer Manufacturing Company, 1960, 94-117; Altair computer, gift of Ivan B. Berger, Laurie Minor-Penland, 88-19284. Both courtesy of the National Museum of American History

P. 197: photograph of Salk by Philippe Halsman, courtesy of the National Portrait Gallery, gift of George R. Rinhart, NPG.84.146. Photo by Philippe Halsman © Halsman Estate

P. 199: photograph of Buck by Clara Sipprell, courtesy of the National Portrait Gallery, bequest of Phyllis Fenner, NPG.82.181

P. 200: portrait of Fitzgerald by David Silvette, courtesy of the National Portrait Gallery, NPG.72.107

P. 201: photograph of Hughes by Carl Van Vechten, courtesy of the National Portrait Gallery, NPG.83.188.23. Photograph © Estate of Carl Van Vechten. Gravure and compilation © Eakins Press Foundation

P. 202: portrait of Twain by Frank Edwin Larson, courtesy of the National Portrait Gallery, gift of Frank Edwin Larson, NPG.72.1

P. 203: photograph of Whitman, courtesy of the National Portrait Gallery, NPG.79.65

P. 204: portrait of Ellington by Gaye Ellington, courtesy of the National Museum of American History, from the estate of Edward (Duke) Ellington

P. 205: Ellington music manuscript, from Archives Center Collection #301, courtesy of the National Museum of American History, from the estate of Edward (Duke) Ellington, Larry Gates, 95-4932

P. 206: Gillespie B-flat trumpet & case, courtesy of the National Museum of American History, gift of Lorraine Gillespie, 1985, Jeff Ploskonka, 86-11768

P. 207: portrait of Gillespie by Marc Klionsky, courtesy of the National Portrait Gallery, gift of the estate of Aron Chilewich, NPG.93.473. © 1988, Marc Klionsky

P. 208: Anderson fur coat, courtesy of the Anacostia Community Museum, Harold Dorwin, 95-015

P. 209: portrait of Anderson by Betsy Graves Reyneau, courtesy of the National Portrait Gallery, gift of the Harmon Foundation, NPG.67.76

P. 210: Davis, *Int'l Surface No. 1,* courtesy of the National Museum of American Art, gift of S.C. Johnson and Son, Inc., 1969.47.55

P. 211: Johnson, *Jitterbugs,* courtesy of the National Museum of American Art, gift of the Harmon Foundation, Michael Fischer, 1967.59.590

P. 212: sculpted head of Chaplin by Jo Davidson, courtesy of the National Portrait Gallery, NPG.72.30

P. 213: photograph of Cody by Samuel Frizzell, courtesy of the National Portrait Gallery, NPG.71.11

P. 214: Indiana Jones jacket and hat, gift of Harrison Ford and Lucasfilm, Ltd., Ricardo Vargas, 92-23; Minnie Pearl's hat, gift of Sarah Ophelia Cannon (Minnie Pearl), 1995, Richard W. Strauss, 95-5509-1. Both courtesy of the National Museum of American History

P. 215: Star Trek phaser, courtesy of the National Museum of American History, gift of Paul Arthur Scheeler, 1987, Richard W. Strauss, 95-5510-1

P. 216: M*A*S*H signpost, courtesy of the National Museum of American History, donated by Twentieth Century Fox, 1983, Dane Penland, 83-7191

P. 217: photograph of Robeson by Carl Van Vechten, courtesy of the National Portrait Gallery, NPG.83.188.39. Photograph © Estate of Carl Van Vechten. Gravure and compilation © Eakins Press Foundation

P. 218: ruby slippers, courtesy of the National Museum of American History, anonymous donation, 1979, Jeff Ploskonka, 81-5294-A

P. 219: Kermit the Frog, courtesy of the National Museum of American History, gift of Jim Henson Productions, 1994, Richard W. Strauss, 94-143

P. 220: Ruth baseball, courtesy of the Museum of American History, gift of Juliana and Robert M. Jones in memory of their father, Thomas J. Jones, 1993, Eric F. Long, 94-13722

P. 221: photograph of Homestead Grays by Charles "Teenie" Harris, courtesy of the National Portrait Gallery, NPG.93.391

P. 222: portrait of Louis by Betsy Graves Reyneau, courtesy of the National Portrait Gallery, gift of the Harmon Foundation, NPG.67.42

P. 223: Ali's boxing gloves, courtesy of the National Museum of American History, gift of Muhammad Ali, 1976, Ricardo Vargas, 93-2009

P. 224: Evert's tennis racket, gift of Chris Evert, 1979; Ashe's tennis racket, gift of Arthur R. Ashe, Jr., 1991. Both courtesy of the National Museum of American History, Richard W. Strauss, 95-5508-6, 95-5507-8

P. 225: Richard Petty's NASCAR stock car, courtesy of the National Museum of American History, gift of Mike Curb, 84-9800/20-A

P. 226: Henie ice skates, courtesy of the National Museum of American History, from Eugene W. Magner and the Sports Illustrated Purchase Fund, 1984, Eric F. Long, 94-9418

P. 227: 1980 U.S. Olympic hockey team jersey, courtesy of the National Museum of American History, gift of Sports Illustrated, 1984, Eric F. Long, 95-5525